Comm-

residents 6 couples + 2 Singles
tent support until health

care cost in maintenance
nexpected need for Nursing
nir to Monadnock –
fit – in all circumstances
RN. ? when do we explai
idents @ early move-in –
dit from monthly fee
N.

intermitent

Printed in China

Big Brown Books
801 Islington St. #35
Portsmouth, NH, 03801
www.browndesign.com

ISBN: 978-0-692-25373-1

FRONT & END LEAFs: Notes from early meetings of
LCSNH. Image courtesy RiverWoods, Inc.

JACKET COVER: Rosemary Coffin and Maryanna
Hatch are photographed in an iconic moment atop
a bulldozer during the groundbreaking in December,
1992. Photo courtesy Ralph Morang.

JACKET BACK COVER: Early LCSNH members
walking the Belmonte Farm in Exeter, the site that
would become RiverWoods.

The RiverWoods Revolution

How Two Women Transformed the Lives of Hundreds

James Buchanan

Foreword by Governor Maggie Hassan

RiverWoods was founded by two amazing women, but they would tell you that the magic of the community has been developed not just by them, but by hundreds, if not thousands of people over the years. From the founders and original consultants to today's volunteer Board members, staff and residents, all represent important members of our RiverWoods community. They have all created a culture of community that is at the heart of who we are and all we do. We dedicate this piece of RiverWoods history to you.

> "We had no money, no deep pocket sponsor, no land. We had nothing – except a dream."

RANNY LYNCH, LCSNH BOARD CHAIRMAN

Table of Contents

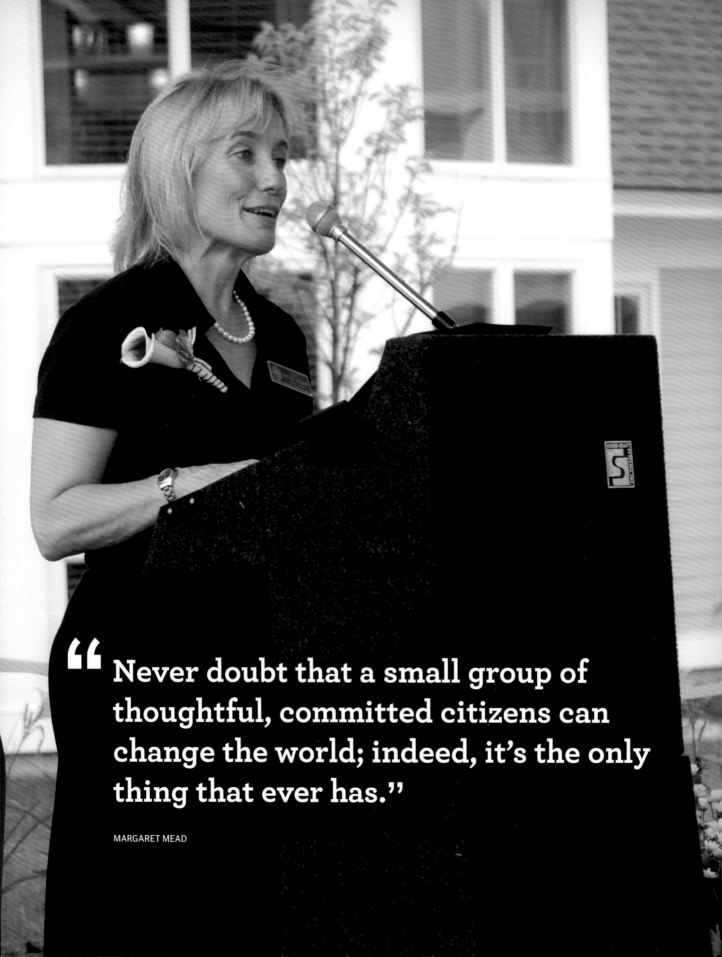

" **Never doubt that a small group of thoughtful, committed citizens can change the world; indeed, it's the only thing that ever has.**"

MARGARET MEAD

The Granite State Spirit

Foreword

Being the Governor of New Hampshire is the greatest job in the world. As Governor, I get to meet the incredible people from all across New Hampshire who make the Granite State such a special place to live, work and raise a family. Our state combines a sense of community and independence unlike anywhere else, and our people are industrious and innovative, while cherishing the traditions that have made us strong. I continue to be inspired by the "all-hands-on-deck" spirit of our people that I see every day in Granite Staters who roll up their sleeves, pitch in and work together to improve our communities.

The grassroots effort that led to the creation of RiverWoods illustrates this spirit and demonstrates the strength and resiliency that define us as a place and a people. Despite the obstacles that they faced, RiverWoods' founders worked together to turn their vision into a reality, proving what is possible with persistence, collaboration and hard work.

I am proud to recognize the work of Maryanna Hatch, Rosemary Coffin and that small band of Seacoast-area citizens who did not give up and persisted to create this extraordinary community of intellectually curious, involved and active residents who now share my hometown of Exeter. Our town and our state are better because you are here.

Maggie Hassan

Maggie Hassan
Governor, State of New Hampshire
April 2014

1

A Kitchen Table Affair

1976 to 1988

RiverWoods is many things. Today, we are 620 residents, 470 staff members and 15 volunteer Trustees. We share a three-campus, nationally-accredited, nonprofit Continuing Care Retirement Community, located on 200 wooded acres in Exeter.

We are mothers and fathers, single people, grandparents and great-grandparents living in a community that enables and encourages us to continue our personal and intellectual growth. We live life on our own terms and enjoy a sense of health and financial security rarely found outside of RiverWoods.

In all, RiverWoods is a vibrant and energetic, self-organized and self-governing community of retirees, staff and Trustees that is a place of opportunity, healing, generosity and giving.

And yet, with all that we have achieved, we are not the product of a well-heeled corporation, institution or investment group. Instead, RiverWoods began its life as an idea around the kitchen tables of Rosemary Coffin and Maryanna Hatch who, with a small group of volunteers, dared to dream of a better, more secure way to live in retirement.

Chellis Associates
Senior Housing Consultants

1982
A mutual friend introduces Maryanna Hatch to Rosemary Coffin, a co-founder of Seacoast Hospice.

June 1983
Life Care Services of New Hampshire (LCSNH) incorporates as a nonprofit organization.

1985
Ransom "Ranny" Lynch steps up as president of LCSNH.

1986
LCSNH enlists the help of Robert Chellis, a consultant with experience creating CCRC facilities.

A SEED IS PLANTED

RiverWoods did not arrive one day as a fully formed vision with adequate investment capital in tow. Instead, its earliest seeds were planted in the mid-1970s as Maryanna Hatch and Rosemary Coffin, independently of each other, recognized that there were serious problems with the way people were cared for as they age.

rather than an enthusiastic choice of where they want to live as they age.

The issue, as they saw it, was that retirees needed a place where they could live when they are healthy, where they could enjoy their lives and make new friends, while having the security of increased care on site when and if they need it.

Personal experience played a key role in inspiring both women.

> We recognized back in the 1970s, that there was a need for something different. So Rosemary and I started talking and everywhere we went we told people that there was this need and that we were looking for alternatives. Well, it got to the point where they were tired of hearing us talk and wanted to see some action.**"**

MARYANNA HATCH, JULY 25, 2013

Maryanna, wife of John, who chaired the University of New Hampshire Department of Art, was living in Durham and raising her family while engaging in extensive community work. Only 20 miles away, Rosemary and her husband, David, head of the Classics Department at Phillips Exeter Academy, were raising their family while immersed in prep school life and the community.

Through their respective community activities, both women reached the same conclusion with respect to elder care. Nursing homes and retirement communities only provided medical care to seniors too ill to care for themselves. In many instances, they viewed nursing homes as places where the elderly are put as a last option

Both had cared for elderly parents and relatives and were frustrated by the cost and lack of available options. As Maryanna noted, "My in-laws lived with my husband and I for quite a long while. I had a pile of relatives living here, there and everywhere, and growing older and finding their lives becoming increasingly difficult. Rosemary, to a certain extent, and in a different way, went through this too. A lot of people I knew had taken care of elderly relatives."

Volunteerism and community service were also important ideals to both women. Throughout their lives, Rosemary and Maryanna were active in numerous causes and projects within their respective homes of Exeter and

ABOVE The original dining room table that served as the first meeting place.
RIGHT Maryanna and John Hatch at the opening of his "Mature Eye" art exhibit at The New Hampshire Art Association in Portsmouth, NH.

ABOVE Durham Community Church, where Maryanna's group first began meeting and discussing a new model for retirement.
BELOW Phillips Exeter Academy, where David Coffin taught and where Rosemary formed her own group to explore senior living options.
LEFT Rosemary and David Coffin were both known for their community involvement.

Durham as well as the greater Seacoast New Hampshire area.

Rosemary, in particular, became intimately familiar with end-of-life care issues in the 1970s, which led her to establish Seacoast Hospice in 1978. This experience of educating the public, organizing volunteers and developing funding for this project proved an invaluable experience during the early years of RiverWoods.

Meanwhile, a few years prior to passage and implementation of Medicaid and Medicare, Maryanna volunteered at a county nursing home here in New Hampshire. This experience made a lasting impression on her as she came to view this type of nursing home as doing little more than warehousing the elderly.

Years later, Maryanna ran for and was elected to the Durham Board of Selectmen, where she worked directly on senior housing issues. As with Rosemary, these previous community organizing experiences were the proving ground that helped the RiverWoods team weather the many challenges it faced during its earliest years.

"RiverWoods is most certainly a kitchen table creation that I don't think was any one person's idea," said Maryanna. "It seemed to grow out of our small group organically. I do know one thing... it's probably the best idea any of us ever had."

In the mid-1970s, as both women became more and more aware of issues surrounding retirement and senior care, they started talking with their respective friends and associates. In turn, they discovered that a number of these people shared the same concerns and frustrations while caring for elderly parents and relatives.

"After talking about this issue for quite some time," said Maryanna, "a small group of friends said enough chit chat, let's see some action." Twenty miles away, in her own world of Exeter, Rosemary and her small band of concerned friends came to the same conclusion: Let's get down to work.

Without realizing that another small group only a few towns away was working on the same issue, Maryanna and Rosemary organized informal study groups to seek a workable solution. Rosemary's faction tended to include people in and around Phillips Exeter Academy. Maryanna's conversations started with her Durham area friends, which led her to form a discussion group at her church.

As each camp worked, they adhered to a common theme of rejecting standard retirement and nursing home models. Instead, they focused on finding and developing a model where people live as independently as possible through retirement and to the end of their lives.

The result was an early vision for a retirement community where people arrive when they are healthy, and have access to future health care support. Importantly, each group envisioned a place that provides made, the newly formed team expanded their efforts and increased their energy to find, research and evaluate alternative retirement community concepts. This included no small amount of on-site visits to a range of

> **Our intent is to provide the freedom for people to enjoy their retirement for as long as their health allows, and then to provide care and community when they need it most."** FRANK GUTMANN, EARLY MEMBER OF LIFE CARE SERVICES OF NEW HAMPSHIRE

continuing care resources so residents can comfortably transition from one level of care to the next as needed, without leaving the community.

Though they may not have been aware of it at the time, both the Durham and Exeter groups had hit upon the foundational structure of a Continuing Care Retirement Community.

Rosemary and Maryanna were trying to raise awareness of the issue, yet each of their groups worked in relative anonymity. They didn't meet until a mutual friend, after hearing both women discuss their ideas on separate occasions, introduced the two in 1982.

Almost immediately, both women's community organizing instincts kicked in and they joined forces that same year.

Once introductions were retirement communities and nursing homes.

"As I recall, we visited a lot of places to see what was going on and very often we were aghast at what we found," said Maryanna, referring to how residents were housed. "Things were very different from what we had in mind."

As they traveled around New England, the small group did not find what they were seeking. The more places they saw, the more convinced they were that they needed to build their vision. With this insight they recognized the need to formalize their activities. In June of 1983, they incorporated as Life Care Services of New Hampshire (LCSNH), a nonprofit organization with Rosemary as its president.

Over the next few years (1984 to 1987) LCSNH added to its official Board roster in

CONTINUING CARE COMMUNITY
TASK FORCE
Minutes of meeting, February 10, 1984

Present: Coffin, Lynch, Brooke, MacDonald, Krooss, Frost
Mary Anna Hatch and Lydia Willits.

Jerry Weiss and Judy Schultz later attended the meeting.

Rosemary welcomed Mary Anna Hatch and Lydia Willits and we agreed that the Durham and Exeter groups would work together. Mary Anna outlined problems they have been having and we told them of our current status.

Rosemary told the group of meeting with architect Jerry Weiss and Albert Bourgeois, who is currently responsible for refurbishing Gorham Hall. She was taken on a tour of the Mill for sale by Nike. Jerry Weiss and his partner, Kent Gilmore are anxious to turn the Mill into a multi-purpose facility which would include a life care center.

Jerry expanded on this idea with a review of the site; its size and possibilities. He spoke of Burt Bourgeois in connection with this. He would seek the necessary financing and will, in the near future, make an offer on the Mill.

Jerry showed preliminary drawings of the exterior of the Mill as possible development which was enthusiastically received by the group. He mentioned that the offer made will be contingent upon acceptance of the projected use to be made of the building. He outlined roughly, the partner-ship that would be necessary to carry through the plan. This would consist of partners who had invested in the project; Jerry as the architect, the contractor and our life care services. They would look to us not for in-vestment necessarily, but for input in the life care section and that our corporation would be responsible for the unit.

A critical factor will be our ability to sell the idea to the townspeople of Exeter. It is thought that the concept of a life care unit near the downtown community has a lot of appeal.

At our next meeting, the group agreed to prepare a question-naire for potential residents.

THESE MINUTES ARE INTENDED FOR MEMBERS OF THE GROUP ONLY

ABOVE Continuing Care Community Task Force minutes of meeting document from February 10, 1984.
RIGHT Pete Richardson and Bill King, RiverWoods residents, kayak on the Squamscott River, past Exeter's historic downtown. Photo Credit: Bill Truslow, Truslow Photography.

What is a CCRC?

Though there is quite a bit of variety among the 1,900 Continuing Care Retirement Communities (CCRC) around the country today, they all seek to serve a similar purpose. Essentially, CCRCs offer a full continuum of care for retirees as they age and require increased medical and related services. Most CCRCs, which includes RiverWoods, are organized into three care levels: Independent Living, Assisted Living, and Skilled Nursing.

In most cases, people move into a CCRC when they are healthy and free of long-term care needs. This is where the benefits of a CCRC such as RiverWoods first kick in. People are freed of the responsibilities of homeownership, as maintenance is covered. They also benefit from one meal a day, housekeeping and laundry services, which allows them more free time to enjoy the wide range of available amenities, services and volunteer and recreational opportunities within a supportive and diverse community of friends.

As residents age and require more care, they are able to transition to assisted living care within the same community where they have established friendships. This makes it easy for friends in the community to visit and allows a spouse to visit often, without having the responsibility of delivering care. Likewise, if a resident requires skilled nursing care they may recover from a surgery within a community that is familiar to them; where their spouse, friends and loved ones can easily visit each day.

RiverWoods residents are guaranteed this continuum of care, paid for by their entrance fee and affordable monthly service fee. Health care will never be denied and will be offered within a warm and welcoming community that they have come to call home. Additionally, with some contracts, up to 90 percent of their entrance fee can be returned if they decide to leave or restored to their estate so when they pass away so that their children and grandchildren may enjoy the fruit of their life's work.

"It was very collaborative. We would meet and brainstorm about what they wanted. Then they passed the hat, tossed in a few bucks and paid me."

ROBERT D. CHELLIS, THE FIRST CONSULTANT TO WORK WITH LCSNH,
IN THE MARCH 18, 2003 EDITION OF THE NEW YORK TIMES

order to create a larger and more professionally diverse group:

- Rosemary Coffin, President
- Martha Byam, Vice President
- Lois Gutmann, Treasurer
- George N. Olson, Clerk
- Maryanna Hatch
- Ransom V. Lynch
- La Ru Lynch
- Prof. Karl A. Pillemer
- Rev. John Lynes
- Dr. Henry Saltonstall
- Frank Gutmann
- Steve Smith
- Dr. Lucius Hill

URGING THE SEEDLING TO GROW

As their research and self-education continued, LCSNH began to embrace the Continuing Care Retirement Community (CCRC) model. However, developing, selling, and constructing such a facility, not to mention staffing and programming the entity, was an incredibly expensive and exhaustive processes.

Contributing to the challenge was the fact that up to this point, (about 1984), there were few, if any, CCRCs founded by grassroots groups without a well-heeled partner. The CCRCs that existed and thrived were the products of large corporations, investment groups or religious institutions such as the Presbyterians, Episcopalians or Society of Friends (Quaker).

Funding for LCSNH primarily consisted of passing the hat during their meetings. In fact, in a 2003 *New York Times* story on RiverWoods,

Rosemary reflects on the early finances of LCSNH and the challenge of finding institutional support, "People thought it was perfectly crazy. Since none of us had any money, everyone wondered how we were going to do it. At one point, I put $1,000 I'd inherited from my mother in the account just to show we were serious."

Additionally, LCSNH did not want to align itself with a for-profit company or investment group. Creating a for-profit entity wasn't consistent with their vision nor was it part of their DNA.

Their first big break came with a chance call between Robert D. Chellis, founder of Chellis Associates of Wellesley, Massachusetts, and Rosemary. Chellis was a consultant in the elder care and retirement community field with considerable experience creating CCRCs, especially for nonprofits in the startup phases of their programs.

"I got a call out of the blue and this woman said, 'Mr. Chellis I'm Rosemary Coffin and there's a bunch of us sitting around our kitchen table here and we want to do a retirement community and are wondering if you could come up and talk with us," Chellis remembers. "All of them were salt-of-the-earth, serious-minded, cheerful people with a vision. It was a real pleasure to work with them."

ABOVE George Olson, early LCSNH member and Exeter Town Planner
BELOW Frank Gutmann (left), one of the early LCSNH members, at a planning meeting.
RIGHT Rev. John Lynes and Maryanna Hatch assess the next step in their plans.

Chellis also notes, "They seemed dedicated to this ideal. I got the impression they were just going to keep pushing it forward a little at a time until they got where they wanted to go. They were likable and wise and they were confidence-inspiring."

In their initial meetings, Chellis helped LCSNH focus their thinking around the concept of a CCRC. The group also developed a formal concept for what they intended to build and the program they wanted to create, which included, "A campus-like life care community. Two hundred fully appointed apartments supported by a service package, which includes: daily meals, weekly housekeeping, weekly laundry services, transportation, social, educational, and cultural activities, 24-hour security, 24-hour emergency call, health and fitness programs, home care services, guaranteed access to pre-paid nursing care..."

Importantly, LCSNH outlined an innovative financial plan that would later prove to be relatively controversial. One of LCSNH's key goals was to offer future residents the greatest degree of financial security possible.

As with most other CCRCs, they envisioned an entrance fee paid largely from the sale of a resident's home to help finance the community. The innovative and controversial piece is that they also wanted to guarantee the return of 90 percent of that entrance fee to any resident who leaves or to their estate when they pass away. "One reason we wanted this," remembers Frank Gutmann, a teacher at Phillips Exeter Academy and early member of LCSNH, "is that we believed that New Englanders

Our Evolving Mission

Mission
1984

"Creating and maintaining a continuing care living and health care plan that will provide financial security when health problems develop and which will help to eliminate the anxiety and fear that often accompany health problems and the financial costs of health care. ….(And by) Providing both assisted and acute-care living in private rooms staffed by health care professionals for persons whose health becomes impaired where a spouse and new friends may easily keep in daily contact to offer encouragement and support during this period of health impairment."

Mission
2013

The Mission of The RiverWoods Company at Exeter, New Hampshire, a charitable not-for-profit corporation, is to provide creative and secure continuing care communities that ease the challenges of aging while enhancing the freedom of senior living.

Vision

Be a leader in providing a superior living experience for a growing number of seniors seeking community and peace of mind.

ABOVE Maryanna Hatch and LCSNH Board Member George Olson in a meeting to discuss the mission.
BELOW Frank Gutmann, a current resident at The Woods and early LCSNH member.

wanted something to pass on to their children and that was a concrete way to build it in."

As Chellis noted in a 1987 feasibility study for LCSNH, "By converting the equity from their home into a refundable entrance fee, a typical retired couple will be trading up from what is simply living quarters to living quarters with desirable services and security features which they might not otherwise afford. It is also attractive to most couples that they will not be separated when the health of one begins to fail. Single people will especially appreciate the chance to socialize, and no one needs to worry about isolation when they are no longer able to drive."

Another innovation proposed by LCSNH was the desire for the community to be primarily self-directed. Gutmann notes, "The high-level concept we wanted to inculcate early on is that residents are co-creators of the community. We didn't want it to be paternalistic in how it is managed."

Gutmann's comments and the early ideals LCSNH members had for RiverWoods reflect not just the ethical context of the founders, but the values that they wanted in a community for themselves as well. They were aging too, and wanted to build a place where they would want to retire to and

live out their later years. The fact that Rosemary and Maryanna, as well as other members of LCSNH, had already lived their lives within a campus setting provided additional confidence their plan could work. At UNH and PEA; disparate groups of people—roughly pulled together based on their academic credentials—managed to create close-knit, vibrant communities.

This early ethos helped establish the cultural and community architecture of openness, resident engagement and transparency that endures at RiverWoods today.

Additionally, LCSNH wanted to offer health care security. In its mission statement developed around this same timeframe (1984/1985), LCSNH declared they would achieve their mission by "Creating and maintaining a continuing-care living and health care plan that will provide financial security when health problems develop and which will also help to eliminate the anxiety and fear that often accompany health problems and the financial costs of health care...

"...[And by] Providing both assisted and acute-care living in private rooms staffed by health care professionals for persons whose health becomes impaired, where a spouse and new friends may easily keep in daily contact to offer encouragement and

" Thank goodness for our spouses. They were so supportive of this effort and the time that we were dedicating to it, but I do think my husband John realized that if he ever wanted to see me he'd have to join our group."

MARYANNA HATCH AND ROSEMARY COFFIN AT THEIR DEDICATION TO FOUNDING RIVERWOODS.

support during this period of health impairment."

As his work with the group continued, LCSNH hired Chellis to research the feasibility of building such a community as well as to add more detail to their plan. After more than a year of work, Chellis presented his report to LCSNH in 1987. In his report, he found that, "Estimates of Rockingham County residents aged 65 and over showed they would need only 1 to 1.5 percent of them to fill their [200-apartment] facility."

He also estimated initial costs to build the facility at approximately $27 million. In the end, it would cost approximately $40 million to build RiverWoods' first campus, The Woods. The discrepancy can be, in part, attributed to his assumption, as noted in the report, that LCSNH would attract

a well-funded partner.

"Successfully completing a project like this as a grassroots group of people is pretty hard," Chellis said recently. "Usually, if a group such as this can get a school to be the sponsor it will work, but that doesn't work out very often. You have to bring the money to the table because schools are very unwilling to spend funds for what they view as non-academic purposes."

Despite the challenges, Chellis's feasibility report indicated there was a defined market need and he encouraged LCSNH to seek a well-funded community partner to provide the necessary financial and institutional resources to make their vision a reality.

A SAPLING TAKES ROOT

In late 1985 and early 1986, LCSNH reached out to Exeter Hospital, Phillips Exeter Academy and the University of New Hampshire as potential partners. With all three of these organizations they saw not only that they shared personal connections, but that each represented a potential perfect fit for a partnership.

To start, nearly all of the members of LCSNH had some connection to either the University of New Hampshire or Phillips Exeter Academy, either as faculty members or the spouse of a faculty member. Additionally, during their research, the group came upon a number of CCRCs that had at an affiliation with a school or university. For example, the earliest communities founded

ABOVE University of New Hampshire (top), Phillips Exeter Academy (center) and Exeter Hospital (bottom) were all approached as potential partners. **LEFT** Robert Chellis was the first professional consultant the LCSNH group worked with in forming their ideas.
Photo Credits: Phillps Exeter Academy and Exeter Hospital courtesy of Exeter Historical Society.

in the Philadelphia area by Quakers—such as Chandler Hall and Barclay Friends —are closely associated with nearby schools and universities. These include the Quaker boarding schools Westtown School and George School as well as the Quaker colleges Bryn Mawr, Swarthmore and Haverford.

Therefore, it didn't take much of a leap to see the obvious potential for creating a sustaining partnership with either Phillips Exeter Academy or the University of New Hampshire.

Given the health care component of LCSNH's mission and Exeter Hospital's community commitment, there seemed to be plenty of potential for a strong partnership between the two organizations.

However, the University of New Hampshire and Exeter Hospital said "no" relatively quickly. While each noted the need for a CCRC and that the LCSNH plan was attractive, neither organization would commit the necessary funds and resources to the grassroots group.

By contrast, Phillips Exeter Academy was rather intrigued by the notion of partnering with LCSNH. As the feasibility study conducted by Chellis noted, "[The Academy] controls several parcels of land not currently required for its academic, housing or athletic programs. The Academy

also has expressed an interest in assisting retired faculty and staff with affordable housing and is presumably not averse to an additional source of income."

Members of LCSNH worked with Phillips Exeter Academy's Building and Grounds Committee chairman, Rob Trowbridge, and committee member Richard Gsottschneider, to identify the most appropriate site. The team came up with a parcel of land located between Gary Lane and the Exeter River. Work between the two organizations went so far as to include topographical mapping and soils testing on the proposed site.

However, the land proved to be too wet for the proposed project and enthusiasm on the part of Phillips Exeter Academy waned. Not long after the mapping and testing was complete the proposed partnership fell through.

As the hope of finding a local partner faded, the group suffered a sad bit of bad luck. For some time Rosemary had suffered from the effects of arthritis, but never to the point where it limited her abilities. Unfortunately, by late 1985 her arthritis became so severe that she had to step down as president of LCSNH, though she remained a member of the group.

Stepping into the role of president was Ransom "Ranny" Lynch.

Ranny was recently retired from Phillips Exeter Academy where he served as chairman of the mathematics department.

ABOVE Ranny Lynch (left) and Dr. Saltonstall (right) in an early meeting.
BELOW Report produced by Robert Chellis.
LEFT La Ru and Ranny Lynch, early Board members. "La Ru came to me and said 'It's time for you to stop doing everything for the Academy and do something for your community," said Ranny, describing how he got involved.

Additionally, his wife, La Ru, had been involved with the effort to build RiverWoods from its earliest days. As it would turn out, he was a natural fit to lead LCSNH through the next few difficult and challenging years.

Frustrated by the lack of a local partner and saddened by the loss of Rosemary as their president, the group was nonetheless resolute in their desire to see their vision come to life. If they couldn't find a local ally, they reasoned, perhaps a like-minded organization within the CCRC field could be found.

As luck would have it, the Kendal Corporation, a Quaker nonprofit continuing care management company, was in the early stages of building its own CCRC in Hanover, New Hampshire.

This development was promising for two key reasons. First, Kendal and LCSNH shared similar visions. Kendal was seeking to create a resident-driven community that could form partnerships with Dartmouth Hitchcock Medical Center and Dartmouth College. Perhaps with Kendal as a backer, LCSNH could overcome the reticence of Exeter Hospital and Phillips Exeter Academy to form strategic relationships with LCSNH.

The second had to do with Kendal's reputation as a leader in the CCRC community. Through their research LCSNH had become very familiar with the quality of Kendal's Philadelphia area life care communities, such as Kendal at Longwood and Barclay Friends, among others. As with the proposed facility in Hanover, the Philadelphia area communities also enjoyed strong relationships with local health facilities, schools and colleges.

With Kendal initiating a project in Hanover it was reasonable to assume that there may be some interest in playing a role in a project in Exeter or Durham as well.

As Frank Gutmann remembers, "We met with them for several months on multiple occasions and some of us went to Philadelphia to look at a Kendal community. At the time we weren't sure what a relationship with them would look like; a developer maybe or perhaps something more or less, but we did have enough organization at that point to know that we wanted to have some local control. So we thought at least we could learn from them and perhaps there would be a great partnership opportunity as well."

Through the winter of 1986 and 1987, LCSNH engaged in a number of constructive dialogues and meetings with Kendal. This led to a number of valuable insights on the design and management of the community LCSNH wanted to build, but it did not lead to a relationship with Kendal.

Ransom Lynch is president of Life Care Services of New Hampshire, the non-profit group spearheading plans for a continuing care retirement community in Exeter.

Article from New Hampshire Seacoast Sunday, August 12, 1990

A place to live (and die) with dignity

Continuing care communities for the elderly are springing up across the nation, and the ground may soon be broken in Exeter for the first one on the Seacoast.

By DAVID SIMS

Maryanna Hatch's in-laws lived in the upstairs portion of her big, white Federalist house in Durham for 18 years. Her husband's mother died at age 93. Her father-in-law lived six months shy of his 101st birth

"They were wonderful people and it was nice to have them close by," she says. But with time, she adds, their illnesses became more and more complex, harder to handle, "all absorbing."

At 67, Hatch is thinking well ahead to the time she and her husband, painter John Hatch, will be able to do less for themselves and will require more care.

"I don't want my two kids to have to take on the added burdens of caring for us with all they undoubtedly have," she says. Involved with issues related to the elderly since she was in college, Hatch has long been active in seeking a way of "guaranteeing care and a quality life to old people."

In these times of staggering health-care costs, single-parent, widely-spaced families and "so many young people simply unable to take care of their parents," the need has never been greater.

Hatch is part of the non-profit group Life Care Services of New Hampshire, Inc., which has been working for years to establish a continuing care retirement community in the Seacoast.

In part, the Exeter/Durham-based group truly believed in the New Hampshire tradition of local control and was very hesitant to enter into a partnership with an entity outside of the Seacoast and state. Maryanna remembers

THE YOUNG TREE IN WINTER

By 1987 LCSNH faced a number of serious challenges.

The group was never well-funded and had no experience designing, building and managing

> " At one point, I was going to night school to complete my degree and my professor believed that by the year 2000 there would be more elderly people in need of care than you could possibly imagine. He was determined that he was going to recruit me to become involved with this sort of thing. Well, indeed that happened. "
>
> MARYANNA HATCH

this period of the group's history well, "We wanted to be more independent and have local control over how the facility is operated, run and governed. We didn't want to join a much larger entity."

They also believed that the flinty New England spirit required an innovative financial approach. "We wanted a significant portion of the entrance fee, it turned out to be 90 percent, to be returned to the resident or their estate and Kendal couldn't buy into that," said Gutmann. "It wasn't part of their way of thinking and financing at the time. They wouldn't budge and neither could we, so that's where we parted company."

a retirement community. Without a financial and organizational partner to help them develop and build their vision, their chance of success was little to none.

Exacerbating their search for a partner was the group's uncompromising adherence to the elements of the plan that they viewed as critical to their vision. For a group approaching wealthy and experienced institutions with hat in hand, their unyielding nature made building relationships that much harder.

However, one set of qualities this grassroots troupe of kitchen table visionaries had in spades was grit, intellect, determination, a little luck and, above all else, persistence.

ABOVE Notes from an early LSCNH meeting regarding the decision to phase construction of The Woods. **RIGHT** Maryanna Hatch with her dog Sophie outside The Woods, near her apartment in Pinkham Village, in 2008.

Architect Chuck Griffin and RLS consultant Doug Powell during one of the early kitchen table conversations.

2

The Improbable Dream Finds a Friend

1988 to 1990

Phillips Exeter Academy, home to half of the founding Board members of Life Care Services of New Hampshire (LCSNH), said "Thank you, but no."

The University of New Hampshire, home to the other half, said much the same thing. It's a great idea, but we are unable to help you at this time.

Exeter Hospital as well as the Kendal Corporation, one of the largest Continuing Care Retirement Community (CCRC) providers in the country, applauded the group's efforts, but said "No thank you."

By this point, mid-1988, Robert D. Chellis, the group's professional consultant in the CCRC field, said he had taken LCSNH as far as he could. "After Phillips Exeter Academy said it was unable to help," he said, "I remember speaking to the group and telling them, 'I'm a consultant and I don't have my own capital to support further development, so what I think you need to do is form a relationship with a developer within the CCRC field. You need one who has capital on hand so that when you find a site that you can either option or buy, they can move in and have the finances to do it. At that point I offered to be available to them, but phased out my work with them."

EGA
ARCHITECTS

1988
Robert Chellis phases out work with LCSNH.

RLS
RETIREMENT
LIVING SERVICES

1989
LCSNH meets with Oakleaf Retirement Services (RLS).

1990
LCSNH signed an option agreement on 83 acres of land in Exeter, NH.

1990
Englebrecht & Griffin Architects of Newburyport, Massachusetts was hired to design RiverWoods.

"They were a very bright group of people with a lot of common sense who knew that life care organizations offered a better way for people to retire and age. They wanted to see one built locally and since no one else was doing it, they wanted to see if they could do it."

CHARLIE TUCKER, FIRST AND CURRENT GENERAL COUNSEL TO RIVERWOODS

Ranny and La Ru Lynch, Rosemary Coffin
and Maryanna Hatch at the Lynch home in Exeter.

Ranny and La Ru Lynch
at their home in Exeter.

Growing Community Support...

During the 1980s many of the meetings of Life Care Services of New Hampshire were held around the proverbial kitchen table. However, as the group talked about their project publicly, more people became interested. Recognizing an opportunity, LCSNH began collecting the names of those who were interested and did all they could to inform and keep them up-to-date.

This evolved into a yearly, open-to-the-community meeting held in the parish hall of Christ Church in Exeter. Here the LCSNH Board of Trustees would report on progress. As more people expressed their thoughts and opinions at these meetings the Board was concerned about having so many cooks in the kitchen. They decided to charge a nominal $10 fee for yearly membership, which allowed each member to vote on important issues.

After a couple of years they collected about $450. This wasn't much money and by the late 1980s and early 1990s, rules for how the Board could and should conduct business became more formalized. The question arose: "What should we do with this modest bank account?"

As a tax exempt, nonprofit organization, they had already stated a desire to ensure the living and health security of their residents. To live up to this goal they used this money to start what has become known as the Benevolent Fund, for residents who may fall on hard times.

Not only did this bank account demonstrate the serious support of many in the community, but it also was the seed for what has become a pillar of RiverWoods' ethos of selflessness.

ABOVE The LCSNH group thought of every detail including signage, parking and lighting for the two entrances.

BELOW Avery Rockefeller's new company, Oakleaf Retirement Services, reviewed the grassroots group's plans and decided to support the project, a turning point in the 10 years of initial work.

THE ROOTS BEGIN TO DEEPEN

With only a few thousand dollars in the bank and knowing they would need at least $27 million, LCSNH began to think about how they could attract a development partner. In this endeavor, they faced nearly the same challenges as with their efforts to partner with the Academy, UNH, Exeter Hospital and Kendal.

They were a grassroots organization without any experience designing, building and running a CCRC and they lacked any significant source of capital. Not only would a developer need experience, they would also need to provide, at the very least, the upfront costs for creating architectural designs, purchasing an option on land and maneuvering the project through local, state and federal approvals.

With this in mind, Lynch called the representatives of Kendal, whom LCSNH had worked with previously to apprise them of the current situation. The conversation is lost to history, but a Kendal representative mentioned there was a development company called Oakleaf Retirement Services that might be interested. It was new to the scene and looking for its first project.

Based in Hartford, Connecticut, Oakleaf was founded in 1987 and composed of three partners, two of whom would come to work directly with LCSNH. Doug Powell had recently left his post as partner in the accounting firm of Ernst & Young where he had been director of its national advisory service for nursing homes and retirement communities. Avery Rockefeller came to Oakleaf after serving within the real estate division of the Connecticut Mutual Life Insurance Company.

Prior to making their introduction to Oakleaf, LCSNH had been busy doing all that they could to demonstrate local interest for the project. This included reaching out to their potential market and raising money through a number of methods. By the time they contacted Oakleaf, they had a list of 200 people who expressed interest in the project and had raised $7,000.

"The first meeting we had with LCSNH was on Ranny's back porch in Exeter with ice tea and homemade bread," remembers Powell. "We chatted for a bit to get to know one another and then Ranny looked serious and said, 'We have $7,000 and 200 people on our list that are interested. Can you make this happen?' We said, 'Let's try,' and that's how it all started."

Though Oakleaf had the Chellis report in hand, the partners felt it was important to perform their own demographic and market analysis. As it turned out, the Oakleaf study came to nearly the same findings as Chellis. If LCSNH and Oakleaf could get just two percent of the potential market within 25 miles of Exeter, the project would work.

The study made it clear to the Oakleaf partners that LCSNH offered a very viable first project for the young company. "It's no question that development capital is a major requirement on a project like this and clearly these guys didn't have it," said Powell. "But after doing our due diligence on the market and considering the people involved—the Board [of LCSNH] was a highly regarded group of individuals in the community who

were credible, honest, local folks—we believed this could work. So we [Oakleaf] raised the necessary development capital from a variety of sources."

They then created a plan for moving forward. Key elements included selecting and purchasing an option on a site, approaching the state for financing via tax exempt bonds, developing detailed architectural blueprints, initiating the approvals process and pre-selling the units.

The team of Oakleaf and LCSNH started work to achieve these critical elements of their plan, many of which had to be completed concurrently. First, two important organizational changes were made. The first was of relatively little consequence. Due to some branding issues Oakleaf became Retirement Living Services (RLS).

The second was more consequential. According to Charlie Tucker, general counsel for LCSNH; Powell and Rockefeller, the two leads for RLS, convinced LCSNH that they needed a more diverse Board. In particular, they needed members with specific legal and financial expertise to help guide the organization through what would be a challenging development process.

"The Board was broadened, but not diluted, and those people who came on really understood the legal and financial issues," said Tucker, a partner at Donahue, Tucker & Ciandella, PLLC, an Exeter-based law firm. Tucker has been, and remains, RiverWoods legal counsel. "Robert [Bob] Field and Collin Scarborough come to mind as

ABOVE Maryanna Hatch, Rosemary and David Coffin, La Ru and Ranny Lynch during a site visit in Exeter.
BELOW Raymond Goodman, PhD, Former Chairman, RiverWoods Board of Trustees.
LEFT Rosemary Coffin, La Ru Lynch and Maryanna Hatch walk the potential plot of land in Exeter.

the most insightful in terms of how to get it financed and off the ground. Bob, because he was a lawyer who had worked on bond issues with nonprofits, and Collin, because he had very acute financial perspectives."

Another astute improvement to the Board, as would be proved later, was the addition of Raymond Goodman. He holds a Ph.D. in Hotel Administration, was an associate professor of Hotel Administration at the Whittemore School of Business at UNH, as well as an active consultant in the retirement, food service and lodging industries. "David Coffin liked to say that RiverWoods is like a cruise ship that isn't going anywhere," remembers Tucker. "It really is like managing a cruise ship so someone with Raymond's background was really important. Once you build it, how do you run it?"

With a new name for RLS and new Board members for LCSNH, the team was ready to begin the hard work of financing, building and opening what would become RiverWoods.

FINDING A SITE

Of all the elements of their plan, selecting a site proved to be the least troublesome.

The primary challenge was finding a site that was properly zoned for the intended use, had access to public water and sewer and was large enough. As Tucker noted, "If you look at the Seacoast of New Hampshire, there aren't that many places that meet the criteria of being zoned for the use, have water and sewer access, are at least 11 acres, and were actually on the market."

Despite these challenges, the team found four potential parcels, three in Durham and one in Exeter. However, there really was no choice. An 83-acre site in Exeter, part of the approximately 200 acre Belmonte Farm met all of their criteria. Located between the Exeter River and Route 111, the site was more than big enough, offered solid ground and had access to public water and sewer. "Fortuitously," said Tucker, "a previous entity had thoughts of a similar facility on the site and had gotten through the preliminary approval process with the town, so it was already zoned properly."

Though the site was on the market, would the owner agree to sell LCSNH an option on the property rather than sell it outright? Maryanna Hatch remembers speaking with the owner one day, "We'd found a space in Exeter that was very interesting and we walked it a few times. On one of these walks we were joined by a fellow

"On one of our walks, an unknown fellow joined us. We walked and talked about the vision we had for the property. Near the end he said, "If you do what you say you want to do, you can have this land."

MARYANNA HATCH

who did not identify himself as the owner. As we walked around, we talked about the vision we had for the property and how important we believed it to be. We got to know this fellow quite well. Near the end of our walk, he stopped and said, 'If you do what you say you want to do and don't bother the edges of the property you can have this land.'"

In early 1990, LCSNH signed an option agreement on 83 acres of the land funded by the seed money from RLS. With an option on the land secured, the team hired Englebrecht & Griffin Architects of Newburyport, Massachusetts, which had considerable experience in the design of CCRCs. John Moriarty & Associates of Brookline, Massachusetts, were brought on as the construction manager.

Hiring an architect meant that it was finally time for the LCSNH's vision to take shape in very specific and concrete terms. According to Powell, it was a meticulous process, "It was a lot of let's look at this and let's look at that and slowly but surely we came to something that was affordable and matched the long-held vision of Maryanna, Ranny and the rest of their group. Also, once we had an architect and construction manager on board, we could do some modeling and studying prices.

"The key was: can we develop

a project that meets the needs of the population, but also has entrance fees consistent with local home values? Typically, a resident sells his or her home to meet the entrance fee and then also has to have enough retirement income to support the monthly fees."

Around this time, the medical expertise of the LCSNH Board was greatly enhanced by the addition of Dr. Henry Saltonstall. A retired surgeon and president of the medical staff at Exeter Hospital, Dr. Saltonstall played a crucial role in planning for the nursing and assisted living facilities.

With a preliminary architectural site plan in hand, LCSNH and RLS, with Tucker as legal representative and guide, went to the town for zoning and planning board approvals. A final plan could not be drafted until these two town boards had their say and made necessary changes to reflect town ordinances and state requirements, as well as mitigated any concerns of abutters.

The process played out in the same manner as nearly any other construction project in a small New England community. The initial plan is brought before the zoning board and the planning board which review it and often suggest, and often require, a number of changes and concessions. The developer goes back to the drawing board and returns with a revised site plan.

ABOVE Dr. Henry Saltonstall, retired surgeon and former president of the medical staff of Exeter Hospital joins the LCSNH Board.
BELOW La Ru Lynch and John Hatch during a site visit in Exeter.
RIGHT Ranny Lynch, John Hatch, and Frank Gutmann walk the Belmonte Farm in Exeter.

WEST VILLAGE

Designing Their Home...

No design detail was too small to be overlooked by the LCSNH Board of Trustees.

Before speaking with an architect for their project, the Board held a number of meetings on their own to talk about what they wanted their facility to look like. As Frank Gutmann remembers, "Most of these early meetings were held at Ranny Lynch's house...he was a good cook.

"We talked about all kinds of things such as what life should be like for residents and what we want in a building. A number of us had worked in schools and colleges and we understood that we didn't

want long corridors, which is why The Woods' main building is jigged and jagged."

The group also talked about a huge range of issues such as how to treat the use of electric scooters. They had heard stories of communities where people with power carts were not allowed in dining halls and other public areas. This meant their mobility and ability to participate in the community was significantly reduced, which is a life changing event. In response, the group wanted a community that could accommodate the full range of modes by which people get about.

River Bend at Exeter

A RETIREMENT COMMUNITY FOR EXETER, NEW HAMPSHIRE
Lifecare Services of New Hampshire
Oakleaf Retirement Centers
Engelbrecht and Griffin Architects, P.C. ©

June 11 1990

They also looked at the placement of laundry facilities. Should each unit have a washer and dryer or would a centralized set of laundry areas help build community? In the end they decided that a communal approach to laundry would be best.

They also discussed pets. Originally they decided that parrots, cats and other small animals would be permitted, but dogs had to be 40 pounds or less. That is until Lynch, president of the LCSNH Board of Trustees, said, "I'm more worried about a 40-pound parrot than I am a 40-pound dog." The group got rid of the size restriction.

More changes are then suggested or demanded, revisions made, and another appearance is made before the board. By the end, if the proposal is for a duck, you hope that what comes out still mostly looks like a duck.

The same was true of the Army Corps of Engineers. They reviewed the environmental and wetland impact of the site and requested changes as well.

In all, it took approximately 18 months to receive final zoning and planning approval. As Tucker noted, "This is partly because it was a big project and partly because this is New Hampshire where it is 'government-by-amateur.' It takes forever because the Board meets once a month

and they aren't paid. Now in Boston, it's worse, and that's 'government-by-professional.'"

In the end, LCSNH and RLS, with the guidance of Tucker, managed to walk away with a site plan that still pretty much looked like a duck.

MANY STORMS YET TO COME

By 1990, LCSNH had managed to accomplish far more than perhaps any other grassroots CCRC startup. They'd found a partner with much needed seed financing as well as the necessary expertise, if not experience, to develop their vision of what a retirement community should be. They had also upped the

professional bona fides of their board and passed through the gauntlet of local and federal approvals for their site and architectural plans.

However, the hardest days yet remained. Securing seed financing was hard enough. Securing full financing to actually build their vision would prove to be a vastly more complicated and perilous journey. The very bonds of the group as well as its determination to see the project through, would be strained to the breaking point.

ABOVE Maryanna Hatch and La Ru Lynch review plans during an architectural meeting.

RIGHT Rosemary, Maryanna and Ranny study plans in a church hall that doubled as a child care center during the day. (top)
The EGA architect reviews the footprint of the proposed building. (center)
Original site plan as proposed by EGA. (bottom)

Site Plan

Rosemary Coffin and Maryanna Hatch are photographed in an iconic moment, atop a bulldozer during the groundbreaking in December, 1992.

3

From Kitchen Table Dream to Reality

1990 to 1995

By 1990, LCSNH and RLS realized that Chellis' initial estimate of a $27 million budget to build RiverWoods was far too low. Instead, they would need to raise $40 million. Private venture capital was not an avenue open to an inexperienced and untested team, especially for such a large amount. The only other option would be via tax exempt bonds issued by the New Hampshire Higher Education and Health Facilities Authority (HEFA), but backed by LCSNH.

This presented two sticky wickets.

The first was demonstrating to the New Hampshire Insurance Department that the project was financially sound. This meant providing documentation for state review of the financial modeling and an actuarial assessment, which required hiring an actuary with experience in the CCRC field. The Insurance Department also had to review the Residency Agreement and the Disclosure Statement to ensure they were consistent with state regulations.

Gaining final approval from the Insurance Department was tedious and took time and resources, but the project was approved in relatively short order.

The second hurdle the team had to overcome was a little more problematic. They had to gain two key approvals from the state in order for the state to issue the tax exempt bonds.

1990
RiverWoods marketing and sales team begin presales on units.

1991
Recession and Presidential Primary causes major stall in presales.

December 1992
LCSNH and RLS hold ceremonial ground breaking ceremony.

August 1994
First residents move into RiverWoods.

"Financing this thing? Well...that's where it really got interesting."

DOUGLAS POWELL, PRINCIPAL OF RETIREMENT LIVING SERVICES

A three-dimensional scale model of the proposed campus was built for the marketing office, which opened in 1990.

> "The fact that we are promised the return of 90 percent of our entrance fee speaks to the intention of the people who founded this place. It's not about the bank accounts of the company as much as it is the happiness and security of the people who live here."

CHERRY TAYLOR, WOODS RESIDENT SINCE 1996

Judy Lamoreaux, Director of Marketing, reviews the site plan with a group of prospective residents in the Court Street marketing office.

The first was with the New Hampshire Higher Education and Health Facilities Authority, which wanted to be sure LCSNH could pay investors back. This meant showing the financial planning was sound and demonstrating there was enough of a market to sustain the project after it opened. The former was easy enough; the financial planning and market analysis performed by Chellis and then RLS were thorough and top-notch.

The latter was quite a bit more difficult. Demonstrating there was a suitable market meant securing a minimum number of pre-sales and deposits on those pre-sales. The criteria have changed somewhat since the early 1990s, but at the time they had to pre-sell 65% of the 200 units. Each presale had to put down a 35 percent deposit against the entrance fee.

Life Care Services of New Hampshire and RLS had to quickly ramp up a sales team. In the fall of 1990, they hired Judith Lamoureux to direct the sales efforts. She was supported by Don Carpenter and Lloyd Darling.

With a clear mandate and time being of the essence, the sales team hit the ground running. They started with the list of approximately 200 interested people collected by LCSNH, and expanded their efforts to include all of New England and beyond. Over the next two years they would send out an impressive amount of well-targeted marketing materials, a newsletter, personal letters and more to prospective residents.

The marketing team also opened a model apartment at 11 Court Street in downtown Exeter. Roy Thomas, a resident of RiverWoods since its opening, remembers, "Of course, back in the early days when they were trying to do the pre-selling for the apartments, the site was still nothing but trees and grass, but they had the office on Court Street that had a model apartment so you could get some concept of what the living facilities would look like and that helped encourage me to come here."

A FEW BUMPS IN THE ROAD

At first, pre-sales were brisk and seemed on pace to reach the target in early 1992, if not late 1991. However, in mid-1991, two external events caused sales to stall and risked undermining pre-sales that had already been made. The first was a recession that hit real estate sales and home values particularly hard in the Northeast and New Hampshire.

The second was the New Hampshire Presidential Primary. Though the Primary would not be held until February 18, 1992, campaigning in the hotly contested Democratic side of the Primary

ABOVE Early advertising for RiverWoods sought to explain the concept and deliver a sense of urgency to potential residents.

Judy Lamoreaux, Director of Marketing and first RiverWoods employee, worked along with a sales team for more than two years in the early 1990's to secure the initial resident sales for The Woods.

Nothing but trees and grass...

How do you market something that doesn't exist yet? How can you capture the imagination and faith of people when your site is, in the words of one early resident ..."Nothing but trees and grass."?

If you're Judy Lamoureux, the first Director of Marketing, you build a model apartment in town and talk with people one on one to explain the process. She describes it this way:

"We had a wonderful information center on Court Street, which was set up so the sales process was a natural flow. We started out just talking with prospective residents when they came in. Primarily, our efforts centered on creating a sense of community, relationship building and helping them think about how good their retired life could be.

"In another room we showed them what some of the amenities were going to be. Then we brought them into a room with a three-dimensional model of RiverWoods, which was a helicopter-like view of what the community was going to look like so they could visualize where people were going to live and congregate and so forth.

"We then walked into a model apartment where people could see for themselves how they could live there. We obviously had to address the fact that this was an apartment, not a beautiful old home, so we helped them think about how they were going to make the transition from their house to RiverWoods.

"As we walked out, we had a beautiful graphic of three women. Many communities had used a photo like this because people would see it and think, 'Oh, the Golden Girls.' At that point in time everybody knew the television show, who they were, and that they were a happy, vibrant group of older women.

"In our conference room we discussed how they could enjoy this lifestyle and that's where we talked about the money, the contracts, the disclosures and all of that.

In all, we gave people a very strong sense of what RiverWoods was going to be, what it would be like to belong to this community and established a relationship with the people who may be residents, even though it hadn't been built yet."

began in early 1991. "The biggest bump in the whole process was the 1992 presidential campaign," Powell recalls. "The country was in recession and Bill Clinton was going around New Hampshire saying, 'We are in recession and New Hampshire will fall into the ocean,' and he's the guy to save us from all of that. Many of the people who were our prospects, and even our pre-sales, heard this and were worried they couldn't sell their homes or wouldn't get anywhere near full value. This put the brakes on marketing."

With marketing slowed, the project, which by now had been named RiverWoods at Exeter, faced three potentially mortal threats. The first relates to meeting the state's standard for pre-sales in order to okay the bond funding. The second was possibly losing the land if they couldn't continue to make payments on the option they had purchased, or the landowner decided he needed to sell when the option expired. The third was concern among some LCSNH members that the project should be delayed, which would have likely led to its demise.

The second of these threats was the easiest to manage. "We went to the landowner," said Powell, "and asked for an extension. He's a very interesting old New Hampshire fellow and he said, 'I've been around a long time and the tide goes out and the

tide comes back again. Just keep paying on your option and it will be okay.' He was very willing to be patient."

To overcome the first threat, the team throttled up its marketing efforts and added a whole new level of creativity. This included a series of events designed to help prospective residents begin to understand the type of community they would move into and feel part of that community.

"We started with those prospective residents who had already signed up," said Lamoureux. "We used some of them in our advertising so people would see local faces or others like them and think maybe this is a good idea. We had community events where we would get everybody together in a local hotel or we would go see a play. We tried to build community and asked each of these people who had made a commitment to bring a friend along. This gave us other prospects we could call."

The sales team also worked to proactively dispel the notion that RiverWoods is just another nursing home. "We hoped that the group events and other community building activities would let the outside world view RiverWoods as a community, rather than nursing home," said

ABOVE Martin Satara, Avery Rockefeller, Doug Powell, and Chuck Griffin at an early prospective resident event, to encourage interest in the project.
BELOW Charlie Tucker, RiverWoods Legal Counsel.
RIGHT Ranny Lynch, Martha Byam and Charlie Tucker during a planning meeting with (below) members of the John Moriarty & Associates, Inc. construction team.

Lamoureux. "It was a challenge to get over this perception. I can remember an article in the newspaper, before we even had land to build on, talking about a nursing home being built rather than a life care retirement community. That didn't help.

talk about how much money you have and how much you will need. It showed that it was still going to work."

The sales team, working in cooperation with the LCSNH Board and RLS, also revised some

> **This is my third attempt to convince the [LCSNH Board] that we are promoting a project that may not succeed. We are asking residents to invest in a big new business in a time of continuing recession and when retirement communities are already overbuilt."**
>
> DR. HENRY SALTONSTALL, JUNE 2, 1992

"We had to be proactive with all of our presentations whether it was to the Rotary Club or one-on-one with a customer, so we created the impression that this is not your grandmother's nursing home."

With the recession hitting property values so hard, the sales team helped people understand the financial implications of their decision to live at RiverWoods. "There were times when people were concerned about their money and we had to talk about it rather than brush it under the rug," remembers Lamoureux. "I remember one woman's situation was that the condos in her development weren't selling for what she thought she needed to get. I visited her and said let's pull out your finances and let's

of the group's policies to sharpen the sales edge. In particular, the contracts were revised to make the initial deposits refundable, which had a huge positive impact. They also redesigned the floor plans to respond to what people were looking for.

In all, the marketing methods created a sense of community among prospective residents and help distinguish RiverWoods as a unique retirement option. "I was living on the North Shore of Massachusetts and saw an ad for RiverWoods in the newspaper and had no idea about it at all. I didn't even know where Exeter was," remembers Ruth Manghue, who moved into RiverWoods on November 4, 1994. "They had a series of meetings, luncheons and gatherings for a number of months before it opened, so we got to know people, and that

ABOVE Avery Rockefeller's firm, now called Retirement Living Services, worked closely with the RiverWoods Board during a crucial point in the development.
BELOW News of the RiverWoods project development was closely followed by local media.
LEFT Dr. Henry Saltonstall, RiverWoods Board Member.

made it very interesting because you felt at home when you arrived at one of these meetings."

Even though the sales team performed yeoman's work to right the marketing ship, it took about a year or so for the economy to turn around. Within this period, sales were not as brisk as they had been and there was some attrition among a few of the pre-sales. This caused some members of the LCSNH Board to wonder if perhaps they should put the brakes on all operations.

In a confidential memorandum issued June 2, 1992, Dr. Henry Saltsonstall wrote, "This is my third attempt to convince the [LCSNH Board] that we are promoting a project that may not succeed. We are asking residents to invest in a big new business in a time of continuing recession and when retirement communities are already overbuilt.

"I, therefore, request that the development process be stopped now and be resumed only when there is a list of applicants who have paid [their] deposit on 75 percent of the units. I am well aware of the arguments against such a decision, but they are not important when compared to the real risk of failure."

This was not the first time this concern had been raised. It was an issue that was debated by the LCSNH Board and RLS through the spring, summer and into the

fall. To say the least, RLS was deeply concerned that LCSNH might choose to postpone, which would likely have meant the end of the project and the loss of more than $1.5 million they had invested. "This was a very uncomfortable time for us because Dr. Saltonstall had nothing at risk," said Powell, "it wasn't his money and our reaction was, if the project stops, it's dead."

This is not to say that Dr. Saltonstall's concerns, some of which were shared by other members of the LCSNH Board of Trustees, did not have merit and should not have been taken up. Failure early would have meant a significant loss to RLS and probably the end of the dream for LCSNH, but failure later down the road would have had dire financial consequences for residents, the LCSNH Board members and, most certainly, to the reputation of the newly formed RLS.

However, RLS believed that the facts on the ground were compelling enough to stay the course.

In response to Dr. Saltonstall's concerns, Avery Rockefeller and Powell issued a memorandum outlining arguments against stopping the development process. Rockefeller was the face of RLS with the LCSNH Board while Powell worked primarily in the background to secure financing and other priorities.

In their memo, they argued a number of points, which included:

— It was normal for startup CCRCs to experience some sales declines and attrition among pre-sales while prospective residents awaited construction.

— RiverWoods to date had not seen slowing in sales or attrition above and beyond what would be considered normal.

— These sales issues were planned for in their marketing plan and budget.

— As with RLS, the marketing firm (Kedney & Associates) was also at risk of losing their fees if the project was stopped and therefore highly motivated to hit sales targets.

— Sales have made steady progress even as their only direct competition (Edgewood in North Andover Massachusetts) had stalled out and despite the recession.

— The anticipated financing structure was geared to protect residents.

— The recession also had a few positives, such as lower long-term interest rates and significantly reduced construction costs.

— The marketing and feasibility research clearly demonstrated the ability of RiverWoods to succeed and there was a clear regional need for such a life care facility.

Rockefeller and Powell also believed that, "Pessimism can, unfortunately, be contagious. The negativism of Dr. Saltonstall's memorandum cannot be allowed to be perceived by the community at large as the attitude of the Life Care Services of New Hampshire Board."

To say the least, said Powell, "We pushed hard on the Board and said we need to stay the course. It took a couple of meetings, but we were able to allay the concerns of the Board and we moved forward. From then on, everyone was completely committed to the process and building RiverWoods."

There was, however, one significant alteration to the plan. Rather than build all four proposed RiverWoods villages—Franconia, Crawford, Dixville, and Pinkham— LCSNH and RLS agreed to phase the construction. The first three would be built when financing was secured and Pinkham would be constructed after the first three were up and running.

"If it weren't for the fortitude of the founders and the development company working together, I don't think RiverWoods would have happened," remembers Lamoureux. "We were trying to get off the ground and were competing with Edgewood in North Andover. They were a much bigger corporation and had a head start, but we were greatly outpacing them to the point where they came to us and asked, 'What are you doing that we aren't?'"

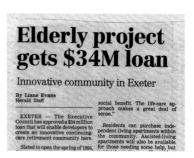

Elderly project gets $34M loan

Innovative community in Exeter

By Liane Evans
Herald Staff

EXETER — The Executive Council has approved a $34 million loan that will enable developers to create an innovative continuing-care retirement community here.

Slated to open the spring of 1994,

social benefit. The life-care approach makes a great deal of sense."

Residents can purchase independent living apartments within the community. Assisted-living apartments will also be available for those needing some help, but

ABOVE State House in Concord, NH, where the Governor's Council met to deliberate on the bond issuance. (Photo courtesy of Gemma Waite French.)
BELOW RiverWoods gets final approval from the New Hampshire Governor's Council to issue tax free bonds.

FINAL STATE APPROVAL

By the fall of 1992, LCSNH and RLS had received permits from the town and Army Corps of Engineers. The financial viability of RiverWoods was validated by the New Hampshire Higher Education and Health Facilities Authority. They had reached the threshold of presales and deposits. They only needed approval from the NH Governor's Council for the issuance of the tax free bonds.

Before this could be given, the team had to hold a public hearing in Exeter, which would lead to their request being placed on the agenda of the Governor's Council. However, according to Powell, local nursing home owners saw RiverWoods as a huge threat and lobbied very hard to try and stop the project.

"On the day of the public hearing," said Powell, "they sent a hired gun lobbyist to the meeting to try and kill this thing. The hearing was actually run by the Executive Councilor for the region, Ruth Griffin, and she asked this hired gun some very pointed questions, such as: "Why are you here? Who is paying your fee?" which made it very clear what was going on.

"Then we had to go to Concord to the meeting of the Governor's Council. We were told by Ruth Griffin that she would try to do this during the executive session of the meeting so that nobody could object to it before we got to the open door portion of the meeting. We sat out in the hall and waited, pretty anxiously, when suddenly the door opened and she leaned out and gave us a nod that said, 'You can leave now. It's all set.' We all heaved a sigh of relief. Thank goodness."

Charlie Tucker remembers Ruth Griffin's political career quite fondly, "She was a tactful politician of the first order. She got things done and got them done quietly, but she got a lot of things done. She was a gem in that regard, not just for this project, but all kinds of things she accomplished. She was good."

On November 19, 1992, final state approval for the bond sale was granted and on December 2,

Ground broken in Exeter

Ceremony held for retirement community

By ERIKA L. MANTE
Democrat Staff Writer

EXETER — Wearing white plastic hard hats and armed with one of many ceremonial shovels, future residents of RiverWoods at Exeter broke ground for the life care retirement community Wednesday morning.

More than 100 people gathered for the ceremony at the 82-acre site off Route 111 which will consist of 162 independent apartments, an assisted living units and a 30-bed skilled nursing center.

The new community, which is expected to be completed in the summer of 1994, will create about 100 permanent jobs and 425 construction jobs.

The master of ceremonies and president of the Board of Trustees for the community, Ransom V. Lynch, told those gathered that all of the necessary permits have been secured, the bonds are on the market, and construction will begin as soon as the financing is completed.

The Executive Council gave authorization for the project to be funded by $35 million in low-cost, tax-exempt, revenue bonds through the state's Higher Educational and Health Facility Authority on Nov. 18.

Councilor Ruth Griffin spoke briefly at the ceremony before picking up a shovel. She said she was supportive of the new community when first approached and that it will be a "whole new way of life for many citizens."

Congressman Bill Zeliff also attended the groundbreaking and said he was glad to be a

☆ Ground
Please turn to Page 2B

Residents Peg Sloet and Barbara Hudson take pleasure in throwing a shovelful of dirt during a groundbreaking ceremony Wednesday for their future home, RiverWoods at Exeter, the first continuing care retirement community to be built in the Seacoast. (Staff photo – Mike Ross)

ABOVE Roz Little, the first resident attends the groundbreaking ceremony for her new home.
BELOW The groundbreaking was covered in the local press.
LEFT Ruth Griffin, Executive Councilor for the Seacoast region, played a critical role in passing the approval of the bonds.

LCSNH and RLS held a ceremonial groundbreaking ceremony. With more than 100 people in attendance, which included state officials, members of both LCSNH and RLS and future residents, LCSNH Board of Trustees president Ranny Lynch announced, "We're gratified to see over 13 years of hard work, determination and creativity finally become a reality. This is an exciting day for us and the town of Exeter."

However, one last hurdle remained before actual construction could begin. The bonds had to actually sell on the open market. Would anyone buy them?

BOND SALE: THE FINAL PANIC

Many of the same issues that bedeviled earlier work to get the project off the ground affected the bond sales.

The recession was still negatively affecting the economy, and LCSNH and RLS did not have a sponsor with deep pockets. This was also the first CCRC facility either group had tried to build. For wary investors, these issues were not reassuring. "In better times and if we'd had a sponsor and more of a track record, this would have taken only about a week," said Powell. "Instead, the actual sales process of the bond took several months."

To handle the bond sales process and to underwrite the venture, the team hired HJ Sims, which specializes in underwriting tax exempt bonds. By April of 1993, the close of the bond sale had to be finalized at HJ Sims' New York office. However, LCSNH and RLS went to the closing without all of the bonds being sold.

"Typically, bond closings are a two day event. You do the paperwork on the first day then have a fancy dinner that night," said Powell. "Then the next day the money goes through. Well, we went to dinner that night having no idea if the money was going to come through and that was a very, very uncomfortable night for us."

"The next day," remembers Tucker, "involved a lot of last minute horse trading. There were lots of last minute deals to get the funding done so that it could sneak over the lines that had been drawn," he said.

Powell adds, "The underwriter worked very hard during this process and managed to convince a bond fund to make some concessions so that we could get the thing closed. This happened at around 3:45 and we only had until 4 to get it done, but we did."

From Kitchen Table Dream to Reality

ABOVE Board members walked through the land and marked trees that were important to save despite the construction.
BELOW Local interest in the community increased when it was learned how significant RiverWoods would be as a taxpayer.
LEFT At long last, in April 1993, construction begins on the site.

WATCHING THE TREE GROW

With the bond money in hand, ground could actually be broken in early April, this time by machines and construction personnel.

By the end of April, site preparations were underway and by summer, work had begun in earnest on the buildings that comprised Phase I of RiverWoods. It was an exciting time for both RLS and LCSNH.

One experience in particular during this time stands out for Frank Gutmann, a member of the LCSNH Board of Trustees. "This is the point where there were marks on the trees and stakes in the ground where the buildings and roadway would be," he recalls. "Some of this land would be clear cut, many other acres were placed under a conservation easement with the town, but there would be areas around the future buildings and grounds where we could preserve particular trees. So about 15 of us went and walked through the building site to find and mark trees that would be significant to be saved...as long as they weren't in the middle of a building."

As a member of the Construction Committee for the LCSNH Board, Gutmann spent a considerable amount of time watching over the construction. "The Construction Committee members would come down weekly and have meetings with our construction manager, as well as supervisors of the various divisions of the construction team. Every week I would walk through the construction site and write down notes and share these with the rest of the committee and Trustees. This went on to where I was no longer walking around excavated earth, but walking through the skeletons of buildings and then the buildings themselves. It was incredibly gratifying to watch it all play out."

STAFFING

With construction underway and running at full steam, LCSNH and RLS now had to hire a staff in time for RiverWoods grand opening in the summer of 1994. This was no small task, as the facility would have 161 apartments, two health care centers as well as spaces for health, fitness, arts and crafts and much, much more. In all, they would need approximately 100 full-time employees.

However, where every detail of the facility had been studied and planned, staffing seemed to come as almost an afterthought. "We really didn't have any particular thoughts other than finding people who could do the job," said Maryanna Hatch.

Asked what the new employers were looking for, Justine Vogel, current CEO and an early

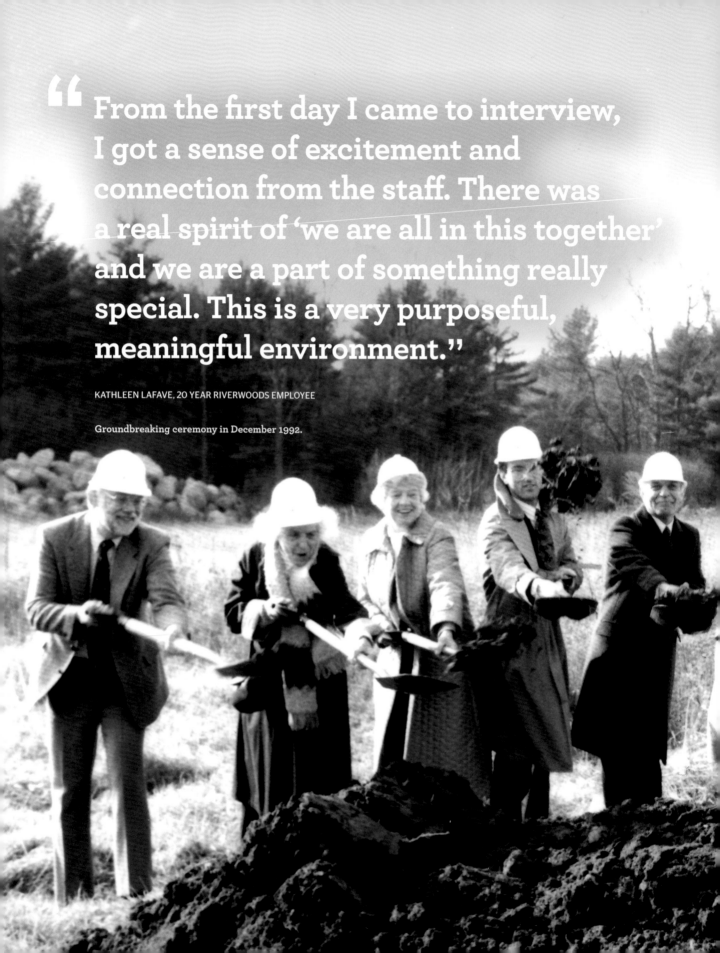

> "From the first day I came to interview, I got a sense of excitement and connection from the staff. There was a real spirit of 'we are all in this together' and we are a part of something really special. This is a very purposeful, meaningful environment."

KATHLEEN LAFAVE, 20 YEAR RIVERWOODS EMPLOYEE

Groundbreaking ceremony in December 1992.

"I started work at RiverWoods on the construction team. When I learned what the building was for, I thought – this sounds like a great idea. I want to be a part of this."

JOHN ISABEL, 20 YEAR RIVERWOODS EMPLOYEE

ABOVE An aerial view of The Woods.
BELOW Garren Henderson, Avery Rockefeller, Rosemary Coffin, Bob Field, Paul Benette at a post-opening ceremony.
LEFT Top above: Top row, (l-r) Celebrating the ribbon cutting of the new building are: George Olson, Exeter town manager; Stephanie Cayten, RiverWoods Board Member; John Settegrin, Marketing consultant; Judy Lamoureaux. Bottom row, (l- r) Rosemary Coffin, Maryanna Hatch, Ruth Griffin, Ranny Lynch, Roz Little, Bob Field and Tom Karnes.
LEFT Below: Chuck Griffin, Maryanna and John Hatch.

employee of RiverWoods, said, "It wasn't prior experience, I can tell you that. There was only one staff member with prior CCRC experience and that was our dining services director. So I can't tell what we really were looking for, but it did seem a little dart board-ish to me."

Of course, it wasn't a careless process either. Rather than seeking people who had spent their lives in elder care, they sought out people who wanted to be part of a community and something new and exciting. "The people who turned out to be successful long-term employees were people who were committed to doing something bigger than themselves," said Vogel, who started out as RiverWoods' Accounting Director. "It wasn't about just having a job. It was about really being part of something special.

"For example, the woman who was our move in coordinator in our earliest years, Gwen Morgan, was able to make a connection with the residents right away, understood RiverWoods is resident driven, and really understood the concept of community. These were the types of people who were successful.

"People who were not successful were people looking to be command-and-control and paternalistic...you really had to be committed to what we were doing."

THE FIRST RESIDENTS MOVE IN

On August 15, 1994, the first residents moved into the newly completed RiverWoods at Exeter.

Roz Little was the first resident to move in and she did so on her 68th birthday. As she remembers, "Everyone here was very helpful and they worked well with the people who were moving in. I also remember feeling excited to move in and that it was a very friendly atmosphere."

Another early resident, Roy Thomas, who moved in 16 days after RiverWoods opened, said, "It was an under-construction-like atmosphere, because they were still working on some of the other units, but moving in felt very comfortable and everyone got along very well."

He goes on to add, "The staff was learning just as we were and there were some glitches in expectations. One thing that sticks out in my mind that helped establish the sense of community was they announced they were going to have dress up for dinner. You know, require people to be dressed formally for dinner. Word got around and there was a resounding 'Like Hell.' This is the first instance I can remember where the residents started to create the community ourselves rather than having it imposed. It represents the way that the community continues to create itself and be a resident-driven community."

Of course, there were some other first-day-glitches, such as problems with the internal phones, a few leaks here and there, and those types of issues.

Vogel was there during those first few days, "I think in terms of early complaints the interesting thing is that we all took the building issues with a grain of salt; it was almost funny. But the fact that the phone system didn't work right, which meant that the emergency call system didn't work, that was a bit more serious. So I do remember when people moved in we gave them two-way radios and said, 'We'll get your phone working tomorrow, but for tonight if you have an emergency you have to call on the radio.'"

Ruth Manghue, another early resident remembers, "It was an easy move as far as I was concerned. I've moved a lot during my lifetime so that wasn't something new and different, but as I remember it was a very easy move. I also don't remember that we really had to do any adjusting to this new community because we'd already met so many of the people who moved in through the various get-togethers they'd organized before the place was built."

A RESOUNDING SUCCESS, BUT CHALLENGES REMAIN

Not only did the first residents move in on August 15, 1994, but a year later, Phase I had achieved a 95% occupancy rate. By that time, Phase II was finished, and with only 38 units, filled quickly. Soon, both phases were at 95% occupancy.

The Woods campus was designed according to some very revolutionary ideas that the founding group identified. First, was light. Almost every apartment has a solarium, a section of the apartment that juts out, bordered by windows, to bring in light. Also, they didn't like long corridors, so the building was designed with turns. Each of the sections of the building were considered "villages" and they bore the names of different notches in the White Mountains, bringing back fond memories of hikes.

Despite much to celebrate, the young community would face a number of challenges in its early history. Not the least of which was a painful rift between residents and the Board of Trustee's leadership and difficult decisions regarding how to ensure the long term financial viability of the community.

ABOVE Roz Little, the first resident to move into The Woods. Her mother also moved into a separate apartment weeks later.
BELOW Residents Buck Hollaman and Herb Jackson clear land among the trees to create one of the many walking trails around The Woods.
RIGHT Resident Herb Jackson strikes a stake to mark out one of the trails.

As a lasting legacy, John Hatch, Maryanna's husband and former head of UNH's art department, painted a mountain scene that now hangs in the entry of the Woods. The two hikers working their way up a ridge in the White Mountains are Rockefeller and Powell.

Woods resident Dot Bell
tends to her raised garden bed.

4

A Single Tree Is Not Enough

1996 to 2004

By the time Pinkham Village opened, RiverWoods had become a living, breathing entity composed of nearly 300 residents, 100 staff, 15 Resident Council members and 16 Trustees, three of whom were residents. In addition, there were health services, numerous resident committees, buildings and grounds, accounting, food service and more to manage.

RiverWoods was no longer a kitchen table affair. There was far more to orchestrate, a lot more at stake and many more stakeholders. Making life more complicated was the fact that there weren't any precedents for how things were supposed to work. Everyone had to establish their role on a make-it-up-as-you-go basis.

As David Coffin, husband to Rosemary, liked to say, "RiverWoods is like a cruise ship that isn't going anywhere." One could add that it's a cruise ship where the staff and passengers have a nearly equal say as the Board of Trustees in how it is run and the direction it should take.

It should come as no surprise that there were some growing pains early in the cruise.

The first of these was the recognition that the current Executive Director of the organization, while skilled at managing the opening of RiverWoods, was not up to the very different task of running RiverWoods. Though painful, the decision was made to seek a replacement.

1996
All three villages within The Woods achieve 95% occupancy.

April 1996
Frank Crane is hired as the new CEO.

1999
RiverWoods receives accreditation from the Continuing Care Accreditation Commission.

October 2004
RiverWoods' second campus, The Ridge, opens.

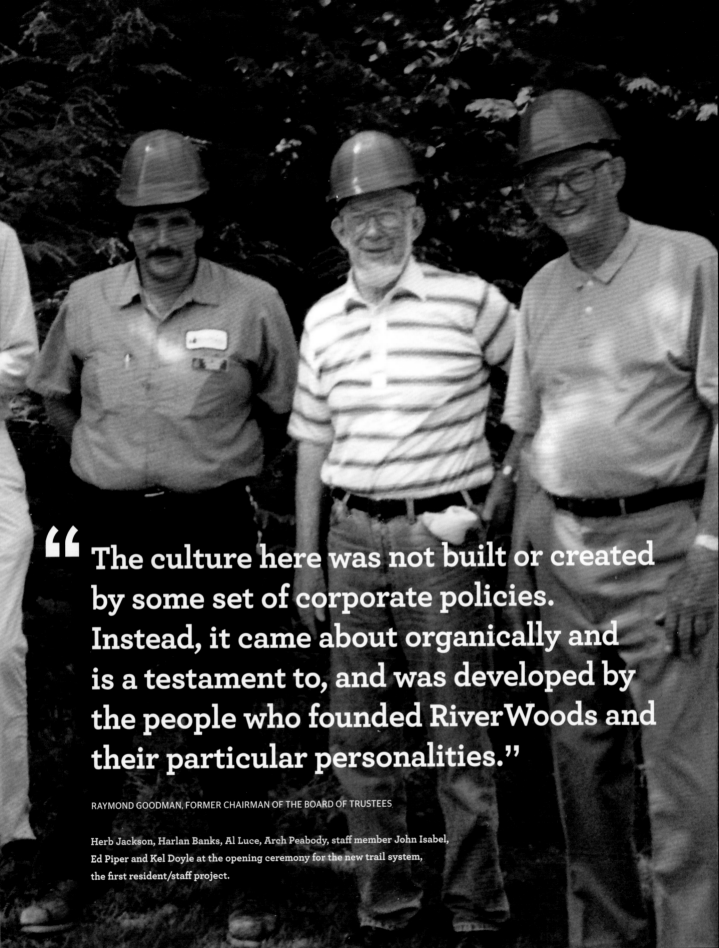

> **"The culture here was not built or created by some set of corporate policies. Instead, it came about organically and is a testament to, and was developed by the people who founded RiverWoods and their particular personalities."**

RAYMOND GOODMAN, FORMER CHAIRMAN OF THE BOARD OF TRUSTEES

Herb Jackson, Harlan Banks, Al Luce, Arch Peabody, staff member John Isabel,
Ed Piper and Kel Doyle at the opening ceremony for the new trail system,
the first resident/staff project.

The Board of Trustees initiated a national search for just the right candidate. After months of looking under every rock and behind every tree, the Board had come up empty. There were a as a hospital CEO. His most recent position was as CEO of a two-hospital system outside of Boston where he played a primary role building a retirement community.

"Henry had gone through all of

number of very good candidates, but not the right fit.

Then one day, while leafing through a stack of overlooked and discarded resumes, Dr. Henry Saltonstall happened upon the resume of Frank Crane.

During the fundraising and building of RiverWoods, Saltonstall had been on the Board of Life Care Services of New Hampshire as its vice president. However, soon after RiverWoods opened he and his wife became residents, which meant he could no longer serve on the Board of Trustees for the newly named RiverWoods at Exeter. He did not stay uninvolved, however. On January 16, 1995, he was unanimously elected to be the first resident trustee by the Resident Council.

Looking at Crane's resume, it was clear he was a very good candidate for the job. He had more than 30 years' experience

the resumes," said Crane, "but for some reason mine had not been looked at before then. Well, Henry gave me a call and said, 'Is this Frank Crane?' and I said yes and he says, 'I have seen your CV and you are coming to RiverWoods. You are exactly what we are looking for.'"

An interview was arranged, then another. If Crane looked good on paper, he was irresistible in person. In April of 1996, Crane became the first CEO of RiverWoods .

His first mission was to establish himself with residents. "One of the complaints I'd heard about the previous Executive Director was that he wasn't very accessible," said Crane. "I noticed that his office was not well located and it was hard to get in to see him. When I got to RiverWoods, I moved my office to the middle of the building and my door was open to anyone

ABOVE Frank Crane with staff member Ray Call.
BELOW Frank starts the first RiverWoods Charity Road Race.
RIGHT Frank Crane, former CEO of RiverWoods.

who needed to speak to me.

"Also, my wife and daughter and I also ended up living at RiverWoods for about three months, which meant we shared meals with everyone at night and saw them through the day. That accessibility meant that they got to know me and I got to know them very quickly."

As he was establishing himself and building relationships with residents, Crane worked to do the same with the staff and Board. However, he ran into the second of RiverWoods' growing pains.

As Chairman of the RiverWoods at Exeter Board of Trustees, Robert Field performed effectively and admirably to secure financing, governmental approvals and work with Retirement Living Services. He also brought a wealth of experience and connections, primarily from his position as an attorney and director of Sheehan, Phinney, Bass & Green, one of New Hampshire's premier law firms.

As fellow Board member Raymond Goodman said, "Bob brought great skills to the initial financing and organizing, prior to RiverWoods completion. He also helped negotiate with several groups, such as the architect, developer and Avery and Doug of RLS. He had considerable expertise working with bonds, which made a significant difference."

Field's style of management, both as Chair of the Board of Trustees and a brief stint as interim Executive Director in the time between the departure of the first Executive Director and the hiring of Frank Crane was efficient, hands on, direct and authoritative. This was at odds with the desire of residents and staff to have more involvement and more access to information. In the early years, as now, the residents desire a high level of transparency with the Board.

In May of 1997, Field stepped down as Board Chair, but continued as Bond Counsel to the organization. Raymond Goodman moved into the Chairmanship role, from Vice Chairman.

With Goodman and Crane in the top spots, RiverWoods began to really find its legs and hit a stride. Justine Vogel, accounting director at the time, remembers, "Both Frank and Raymond had a philosophy that was very collegial and things just really took off because we had the right residents, the right leadership on the Board and the right leadership on the staff. Everything just clicked and the relationship between staff, Board and residents was cemented."

It was so good, in fact, that this relationship has come to be known as the Three Legged Stool.

ABOVE RiverWoods residents made it a practice to raise money and donate time to many area nonprofits, including Seacoast Hospice, New Teen Outlook Center and painting a mural at the Exeter Town Pool as part of Planet Playground.
RIGHT Sally Hollaman, Bob Lietz, and Justine Vogel representing the Three Legged Stool, comprised of resident, Board and staff.
Photo Credit: Joanne Smith, Headshots Photography.

Three Legged Stool

The seeds of the Three Legged Stool were planted when the founding members made the conscious decision to create a resident-driven community. From the very beginning, the grassroots group wanted to create a community that they would be active partners in and that concept grew more rooted as the RiverWoods organization was formed. Their goal was that the Board of Trustees, staff and residents should work together to create community, solve problems and seek ways to make RiverWoods even better.

During RiverWoods' early days, the concept of a Three Legged Stool came to life as residents requested greater transparency and energetically worked with staff and Board to define the life they desired. It really took shape when the community came together during RiverWoods' first formal accreditation process. The Board, staff and residents worked collaboratively for many months to respond to the detailed accreditation requirements established by the Continuing Care Accreditation Commission. With a shared goal and distributed responsibilities, RiverWoods forged a real and highly effective Three Legged Stool.

To many, the Three Legged Stool is what makes RiverWoods unique. As Justine Vogel, CEO and President of RiverWoods said in a May 2012 issue of Business NH Magazine, "What's really different is we actually care what residents think. Residents want someone who is their partner, not their parent. Their input matters in every decision we make."

Former Board of Trustees Chair, Raymond Goodman, agrees, saying, "RiverWoods is completely transparent, which is atypical from what I see in the industry even now. Typically, Boards are very removed from the community and focus exclusively on policy, whereas The RiverWoods Board is open, transparent and available to the community."

When Frank Crane, former CEO of RiverWoods, was asked to describe the spirit of RiverWoods, he said, "It's the Three Legged Stool. It typifies the spirit and inspires it."

KEEPING THE TREE HEALTHY AND STRONG

With the Three Legged Stool in place, Crane could spend more time focusing on the day-to-day management of the community. This was something of a two-fold challenge.

The first related to issues of individual residents, such as problems with their homes, concerns over certain policies and ensuring the entire staff were delivering on the best possible experience for residents. It probably isn't too surprising that this aspect of Crane's job ran the gamut from troubleshooting and dining complaints to helping residents work through their personal relationships.

"You never know what each day will bring. One day, a guy came into my office and said, 'I'm like a teenage kid. I'm in love and I don't know which way is up or if I'm going back or forward or what.' I smiled and told him I couldn't offer much advice on matters of the heart, but I did tell him not to combine their assets or your kids would kill you."

Crane's second challenge, equally as important as the first, was to ensure the long-term financial success of RiverWoods. As he would find out, this was a bit more of a challenge than he anticipated.

THE TREE IS HEALTHY AND SOUND

In the world of Continuing Care Retirement Communities (CCRCs), there is a national accreditation body, called the Continuing Care Accreditation Commission (now known as CCAC/CARF). Accreditation by this organization is the equivalent of the Good Housekeeping Seal of Approval. It demonstrates the overall health of the CCRC.

Typically, because accreditation involves demonstrating significant financial strength, a community will wait many years before even applying. In 1999, with less than five years of operation, RiverWoods became one of the youngest organizations to apply.

After April 1997, things at RiverWoods really started to click. Relationships between Board, staff and residents were strengthening each day. Problems were not only being solved, but anticipated and mitigated. The community expanded to include an ever-growing number of services and activities to residents. And occupancy was at 98%, which is exceptional in the industry.

However, both Crane and Vogel agree that RiverWoods didn't really blossom until it began the process of accreditation. "The first accreditation was in 1999," said Vogel, "so what you had was this period after 1997 where things are getting better, but we really

ABOVE Members of the national CARF Accreditation Survey Team during their first on site survey visit in 1999.
BELOW RiverWoods was one of the earliest communities to achieve national accreditation.
RIGHT The CCAC Surveyor presents CEO Frank Crane and resident Al Kuusisto with the formal accreditation certificate.

hadn't coalesced. Then, in the course of the next year, we started working on our accreditation. In those days, to get accredited you had to write answers to hundreds of questions, which represented about a three-inch notebook worth of information. Then they would come in and evaluate you for EVERYTHING."

Obviously, this was no small amount of work. To manage it all, they broke the project into a set of discrete tasks overseen by an accreditation team composed of residents, Board members and staff. Vogel explains, "We had this team write and edit the document."

Then RiverWoods prepared for the site visit. "It is a peer evaluation, basically," said Crane. "What it

meant is that we had to ensure our finances were in good order and that we are delivering on all of the services we promised and that we are meeting the strict national requirements of the CCAC.

"Well, when the accreditation team came through, they were dumbfounded. It was clear that we—the residents, staff and Board—were a team and that we really, truly care for the community we were in the process of creating. It was an unbelievable thing to see...it really was."

At the conclusion of the three-day site visit, there is an exit meeting with the CCAC site surveyors. "Usually, this is done with just a handful of

representatives of the community, but Frank [Crane] said, 'No, we did this work together so let's do this meeting together, with our residents and everybody else." The Great Bay Room of the Woods campus was packed with 100 residents and staff.

"There are about 30 standards we had to meet," said Vogel, "and as they read the standard and then recited their response, 'The standard is met,' a cheer would erupt. This happened for all 30 of the standards. And then they noted all of the things we received exceptional commendations for and people cheered for that too.

"It was a feeling of togetherness and we were all proud of our

Worth Waiting For

Yes, it does happen. The RiverWoods community creates new friendships and sometimes even new love. Perhaps one of the loveliest of these stories is that of Nancy Alcock Hood and Henry Hood.

"I was not upset that I'd never married," Nancy said. "I'd never met anyone I thought to be with for the rest of my life, until I met Henry. He was worth waiting for."

Henry moved to RiverWoods with his first wife in 2003 and she unfortunately passed away only a few months later. At the time, Nancy was chair of the Resident Council and noticed how bereft he was. "I thought it would be good to get him involved."

After becoming friends while working in the Council, they found they had a lot in common. Before long, the two had fallen in love and were married at the Cathedral of the Pines in Rindge, NH in 2008 with his children and grandchildren in attendance.

Sadly, Henry passed away in the winter of 2012. "I miss Henry terribly, but we had four-and-a-half years together and they were really wonderful years. I'm very thankful for that."

"The thing I will never forget is the first day we came back from our brief little honeymoon, we walked into the dining room and everyone clapped."

NANCY ALCOCK HOOD ON RESIDENTS' REACTION TO HER WEDDING

community. I remember the feeling like it was yesterday."

The Woods, we had a larger number of smaller units and a smaller number of large units. This was a problem.

> " At one meeting with the Resident Council, Frank Crane explained why expansion could be helpful. He really laid it out. For many residents it was a leap into the unknown, but the process was very open and there was no secretiveness about the idea. "
>
> DICK APLIN, WOODS RESIDENT SINCE 1995

A LONE TREE WILL PERISH

Accreditation gave RiverWoods its gold seal of approval and solidified its reputation. However, it didn't assure the long-term fiscal health of the organization. In fact, there were problems.

After accreditation, if not before, Crane and Goodman recognized they had to invest time examining the long-term viability of the community, which led them to an industry conference in 2000. "We went to a senior living industry conference sponsored by our investment banker," said Goodman. "We both left that conference and looked at each other and said, 'We have to grow.'"

Prior to the conference, intuition drove concern. After the conference and an examination of the structure of RiverWoods, both men implicitly understood that RiverWoods' fiscal health was not as strong as they hoped.

As Goodman explains, "At the time, with just the one campus,

"With the imbalance of large to small units we couldn't get enough monthly income to cover the operations. What we did was cover the deficit with some of our investment income and entrance fees."

Although it was not an atypical practice for CCRCs, the challenge of relying on investment income and entrance fees was not sustainable for the long term. This strategy was also risky because RiverWoods' investment income was susceptible to market shifts, corrections and recessions. "When we realized this," said Goodman, "we knew that growth was essential to ensure our financial strength."

"There was another reason: RiverWoods is a good idea and it is part of our mission statement to make RiverWoods available to more people. So, how can we do that?"

Now all they had to do was convince the Board, staff and residents. Not an easy job.

ABOVE Raymond Goodman, as Board Chair, kept residents in the loop with regular meetings about the concept of expansion.
BELOW A momentous occasion - RiverWoods breaks ground for The Ridge, its second campus.

RiverWoods Core Values

One challenge of growth the RiverWoods team found once the Ridge was opened, is that more people had to be hired. Now that the pace of hiring sped up, there wasn't always a great match.

Frank Crane hired Bruce Mast and Associates to help the RiverWoods leadership team define the qualities that would make a good employee. The team worked for several hours during an off-site retreat, examining what was at the core of the philosophy that made certain employees flourish.

The end result is now known as the "RiverWoods Core Values," and they are a key component of creating the community. The values have endured and are part of an employee's performance review and evaluation. The values are:

— Respect for the individual
— Authenticity
— Not for self
— Mutuality
— Sustainability

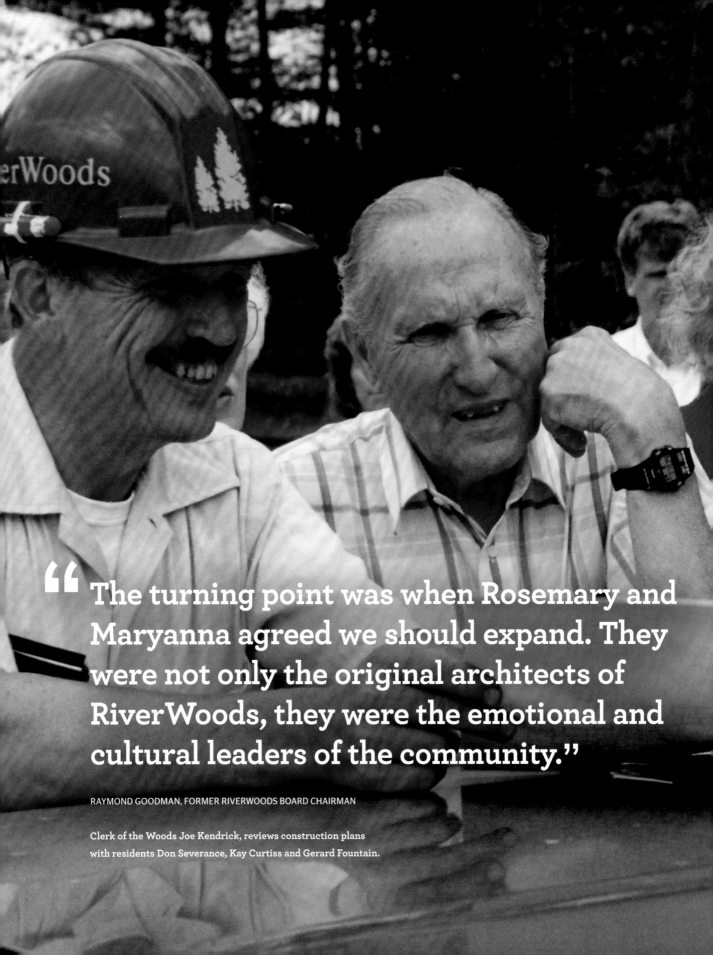

"The turning point was when Rosemary and Maryanna agreed we should expand. They were not only the original architects of RiverWoods, they were the emotional and cultural leaders of the community."

RAYMOND GOODMAN, FORMER RIVERWOODS BOARD CHAIRMAN

Clerk of the Woods Joe Kendrick, reviews construction plans with residents Don Severance, Kay Curtiss and Gerard Fountain.

"We met an enormous amount of resistance when we announced our intention to grow," said Goodman. "We met resistance from the residents. We met resistance from the founders. We met resistance from some members of the Board."

In fact, even the very first founders of RiverWoods, Rosemary Coffin and Maryanna Hatch, required convincing that the community should grow to include an entirely new campus.

In all, the resistance came down to two primary concerns. The first; Will we break this wonderful culture and way of life if we add on to it? "'We like the way it is now and if we grow, we won't be the little community that we love, and the culture we've developed won't be the same if we allow more people here,'" remembers Goodman. "And the Board also shared this mindset."

The second concern was, if whatever we add fails, we'll all go belly up. As Crane remembers, "Residents were worried about RiverWoods over-extending itself. They worried, 'If this thing goes down the drain what are we going to do? I will turn 75 in a couple of weeks and I have my finances relatively in line, but I would be devastated if this project falls through.' Others worried that we were simply being egotistic and over-extending ourselves."

Goodman and Crane were confident they were on the right

ABOVE Phebe Terrell, a current Ridge resident, poses before a construction sign during a preliminary visit to the site. **BELOW & LEFT** RiverWoods innovated with the opening of The Ridge, by adding 11 cottages to the apartment mix, separate but adjacent to the main building.

path. Except for a handful of people, they had to convince everyone else. Not surprisingly, they did their homework and began to educate everyone on what they found. This included two market feasibility studies. One was done by Greystone Communities, Inc., a national development company in the senior living industry.

In early days of planning the Ridge expansion, the Board seriously considered joining a national system instead of growing on their own. The idea was that being part of a larger, financially-secure organization would offer the long-term financial security RiverWoods sought.

However, financial security would have come at a cost. As Goodman pointed out, being part of a larger national system would have cost RiverWoods upward of $500,000 per year.

"We were already in operation and had survived the initial start-up risk factor, so why would we then want to support another organization and its goal to expand their product?" asked Goodman.

If the plan to expand moved forward, Greystone would most likely be the development partner. With a belt-and-suspenders mindset, they commissioned a second report from a national firm, the ProMatura Group, which was done by Dr. Margaret Wylde.

These reports, plus the success of RiverWoods demonstrated that the community faced a further financial risk.

"At the time, we had a five year wait list, which meant we had latent demand," said Goodman. "If you have latent demand you are inviting competitive entry. If we build and absorb that latent demand we will lock out competition."

Both feasibility studies all but assured the success of building a second campus. This information enhanced education efforts. "I am not the kind of CEO to say I know everything so we brought in experts, auditors and others to tell residents, staff and Board members what is going on in the senior living business and why growing made sense. I also took residents and staff to trade association conferences to see for themselves what is happening in our business. So I brought in people to head up all of these efforts who knew what it is all about."

As members of the Board and Resident Council started to see the need for growth, they became evangelists to the rest of the community for the need to build a new campus. It was a relatively slow process, but one where persistence paid off.

Perhaps the most significant turning point, said Goodman, was

RiverWoods at Exeter opens new neighborhood: 'The Ridge'

EXETER — RiverWoods at Exeter recently commemorated the opening of its new neighborhood, The Ridge, with a celebratory ribbon cutting.

Raymond J. Goodman, Jr., Chairman of the RiverWoods Board of Trustees, opened the ceremony with congratulatory remarks. The ribbon cutting was well attended by Exeter Area Chamber of Commerce ambassadors, RiverWoods Board of Trustees and Resident Council members, and representatives of The Ridge's development, construction and architectural firms.

The new Ridge campus is located across Route 111 from the RiverWoods neighborhood. The Ridge adds an additional 81 independent living apartments, 11 cottages and its own Health Center (which includes assisted living and skilled nursing care), to the 200 independent living apartments and health center at the original RiverWoods campus.

The Ridge officially opened Oct. 25, when it welcomed its first eight residents, who hailed from as close as Nottingham, N.H., and Rockport, Mass., to as far away as Pennsylvania and Florida.

ON NOV. 3, the ribbon cutting for the new RiverWoods development was attended by: Front row, from left, Raymond J. Goodman Jr., chairman of the RiverWoods Board of Trustees; Jane McCarthy, chair of the RiverWoods Reporter newsletter; Dr. Nancy Alcock, RiverWoods Resident Council member; Frank S. Crane III, president/CEO of RiverWoods; Justine Vogel, RiverWoods senior vice president; and Robin Tufts, of JSA, Inc. Second row: Anthony Codding and Richard Siener, RiverWoods trustees; Dr. Henry Hood, vice chair of the Resident Council; and Allan Prince, chair of the RiverWoods Resident Finance Committee. Other rows are filled with representatives of the Exeter Area Chamber of Commerce, LeCesse Construction Company and Greystone Communities, Inc.

Project contractor is LeCesse Construction Company; development consultant is Greystone Communities, Inc., and architect is JSA, Inc. For more information about The Ridge at RiverWoods, contact Maria Hutchings at 603-658-1500.

ABOVE & RIGHT Construction begins on The Ridge, RiverWoods' second campus, on a parcel of land across the road from The Woods. **BELOW** Raymond Goodman, Nancy Alcock, Henry Hood, Frank Crane and Justine Vogel are pictured at The Ridge grand opening.

when Maryanna and Rosemary came to see his and Crane's point of view. "Because of who they are and their role as the original architects of RiverWoods' cultural ethos, they were the emotional and cultural leaders of the community. When they recognized the need for us to grow...well...that was an important moment," he said.

In the end, staff, residents and most of the Board were convinced that RiverWoods needed to do this, and needed to do this now. "The Holloway and Bennett families owned adjacent tracts of land which totaled 109 acres, across the street from the current location and the price was right," said Goodman.

As with the original campus, The Woods, the group sought bonds underwritten by the state. Unlike the first time, they now had a track record, income, and initial investment capital so there was little for the state and the bond market to object to. The bond was approved.

A NEW TREE TAKES ROOT

On October 25, 2004, The Ridge opened. In one fell swoop RiverWoods had doubled the amenities it offered; adding 81 apartments, 11 cottages, a 27-bed assisted living facility and a 23-bed skilled nursing care facility, dramatically increasing the size of its resident population.

The project had achieved 95% pre-sales prior to the construction, and, happily, the building filled quickly, proving that RiverWoods' concept remained popular, and ensuring increased revenue. "The facts bore out the findings of the feasibility studies we produced, as well as our gut instincts," said Goodman. "Within a year of opening we reached stabilized occupancy, which helped us get to break even."

However, challenges remained. As the Board and staff were to find out, their assumption that The Ridge would be just another community was way off base. The success of The Ridge also demonstrated that RiverWoods had not yet taken up the latent demand for CCRCs on the New Hampshire Seacoast. The area was still ripe for a competitor—perhaps a large one with deep pockets—to move in. Worse yet, the national and world economies were on the verge of experiencing the most devastating real-estate-driven financial slide since the Great Depression.

In the midst of all this, the community would have to say goodbye to its beloved CEO.

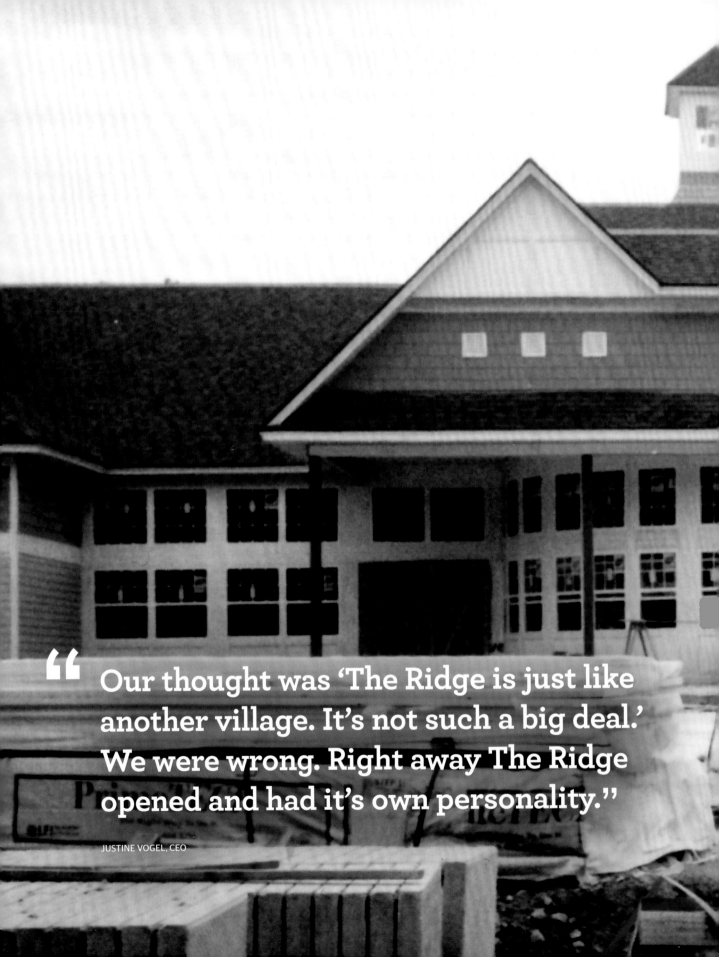

"Our thought was 'The Ridge is just like another village. It's not such a big deal.' We were wrong. Right away The Ridge opened and had it's own personality."

JUSTINE VOGEL, CEO

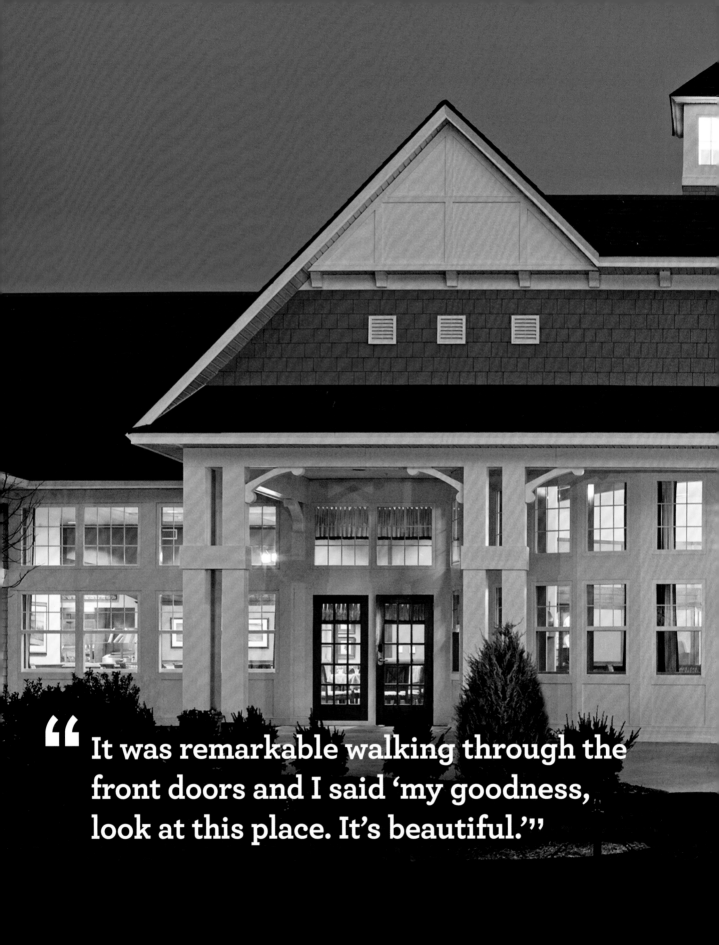

"It was remarkable walking through the front doors and I said 'my goodness, look at this place. It's beautiful.'"

RiverWoods residents Walter Sanderson, Richard Fitts, William Vogel, Hollis Caswell and Richard Sargeant spend a day with local boys from New Teen Outlook Center on a joint project of building a picnic table

5

Like No Other Community

2005 to 2014

As new residents begin to stream into The Ridge, it soon became apparent that RiverWoods had not cloned The Woods. Instead, The Ridge residents felt that they wanted to create their own identity, separate from The Woods.

As Justine Vogel, CFO of RiverWoods at the time, remembers, "I take responsibility for this, but our thought was, 'The Ridge is just another village. It's not such a big deal.' Wrong. The Ridge opened and right away it had its own personality."

Of course, the underlying cultural architecture of open, resident-driven community building that The Woods had was one of the aspects that attracted the new residents. Perhaps that is why they were so intent on creating and defining their own community as well.

Given this natural proclivity toward independence, it wouldn't have been surprising if these two communities had spun off in their own directions in the same manner as two alienated siblings. They would share the same DNA, but live their lives as separate individuals.

The most significant factor preventing a fraternal split and creating a true familial bond during those early days was the welcoming they received from Woods residents, and

2005
Occupancy for both The Woods and The Ridge reaches 95%.

2007/2008
Justine Vogel becomes CEO. Bob Lietz becomes Chairman of the Board.

2008
Construction begins on RiverWoods' third campus, The Boulders.

March 2010
The Boulders opens and achieves 80% occupancy in the first 3 months.

then chairman of the Resident Council, Henry Hood. Henry took it upon himself to personally welcome nearly every new resident of The Ridge.

A SEASON OF CHANGE

By 2005, The Ridge and The Woods were humming along. Occupancy for both campuses was up around 95%. Issues related

> " When we first got here The Woods people said: 'We'll be in charge and you can be on the committee.' I don't think they realized that each RiverWoods community wants their own space and they want their own events and they want to be in charge of their own campus. "

LORRAINE GRAHAM, ONE OF THE FIRST RIDGE RESIDENTS

He also presented them with a handbook of sorts that the residents had written that laid out some of the culture and traditions that had evolved at RiverWoods. Its title was *The Pleasures of RiverWoods*.

"We still give this book out to all new residents when they arrive," said Cathleen Toomey, Vice President of Marketing. "Henry, who was a retired neurosurgeon, met with all of the 'Ridgies' who moved in. He talked with them and gave them the book that described all of the great things about RiverWoods. That's community…what he was doing was spreading community."

"However," adds Toomey smiling, "we did change the title because the original title seemed a little X-rated."

Frank Crane, RiverWoods CEO at the time, adds, "Henry, as an army of one took on the issue of bringing The Ridge into the community of RiverWoods."

to transitioning to a two-campus community were largely ironed out, savings and investments were secure and RiverWoods had reached a state of financial stasis. Additionally, the community was accredited, had been named Business of the Year by *NH Business Review*, won awards for the designs of its campuses and been named "A Best Place to Work."

In other words, it was a great time for Crane to begin making noises about retiring.

When Crane arrived at RiverWoods it could easily be said that the community was in a state of upheaval; it had not yet unified into what would become The Three Legged Stool. With Raymond Goodman, the new Chair of the Board of Trustees, they were able to turn all of that around. Working hand-in-hand and, with all of the stakeholders, Crane and Goodman built what had become a fully functioning,

ABOVE Frank and Lorraine Graham, early Ridge residents.
BELOW Marilyn Wentworth, a Ridge resident who published a book with two other residents.
LEFT Tom Adams, Ridge resident, former physician and master potter at work in the Ridge pottery studio.

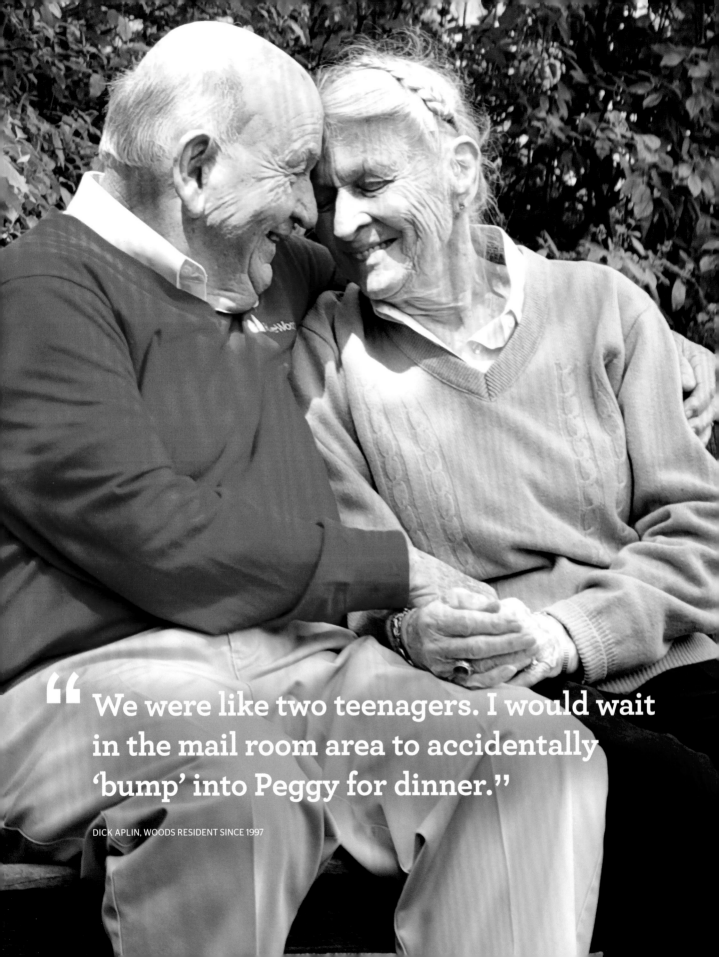

> "We were like two teenagers. I would wait in the mail room area to accidentally 'bump' into Peggy for dinner."

DICK APLIN, WOODS RESIDENT SINCE 1997

A RiverWoods Love Story

When residents move to a retirement community, they expect to meet new people, become involved in new activities and enjoy more free time. But sometimes, the unexpected happens.

Take the case of Dick Aplin. He moved to RiverWoods in 1997, with his wife JoAnne. In time, JoAnne became ill and Dick cared for her lovingly until her passing.

Dick, who was an active member of the Resident Council, took the time to meet all new residents. But one night, soon after his wife died, a sparkly eyed woman, Peggy Hoyt, was seated at his table, and he knew this was different.

Peggy, an independent woman had motorcycled across the country, lived many places, and had a feisty repartee that matched Dick's wit. Soon, Dick started to hang around the mail room, so he could "happen" to run into Peggy. A first date at The Old Salt followed, and soon they were keeping company.

"I was nervous to tell the kids," says Dick. "One Christmas I was visiting my son in Colorado, and I wanted to call Peggy, so I took the phone outside to make a call, and whispered." Peggy was impressed. "We grew up when long distance calls were a lot of money. I thought, he must be serious if he called me from far away."

Their connection was strong, and soon they met each other's families, and got the approval of the kids, and had a beautiful wedding in the Great Bay Room at The Woods. Several hundred attended and it only strengthened the community bond that brought two people together.

cohesive community with a top-notch and well-oiled management team.

Upon his arrival, Crane had already logged more than 30 years as a successful hospital CEO. He was an experienced manager and leader, and he understood the concept of community and how to build it. He was also near the end of his career. By 2005, he was ready to enjoy the rewards of his years of hard work. Before he did, however, he wanted to ensure that all of RiverWoods' achievements and momentum, much of which he'd played a large part in creating, would not evaporate after he left.

Adding to the dilemma was the fact that Goodman was also nearing the end of his term and close to retiring from the Board. Goodman's resume was as strong as Crane's and his personality was a natural fit with Crane's and that of RiverWoods' founding ethos.

With these two important leadership posts in transition, RiverWoods faced a significant test. Did RiverWoods' strength depend on the leadership of these two? After all, far too many organizations have failed because they were built around a single personality or set of personalities.

Or, are the core principles that RiverWoods is built on—its cultural architecture (e.g. The Three Legged Stool)—strong enough to outlast any single leadership team

and endure into the future?

The first step took place when Crane reached out to Goodman. As Goodman remembers, "Frank and I made the decision that we wouldn't retire at the same time, so there would be some overlap. We didn't want to leave without some form of leadership continuation."

The second step was finding a new CEO with the right mix of personality and leadership traits to ensure their success, continued success of the community and a smooth transition. As it turned out, Crane and Goodman (as well as the Board of Trustees and Resident Council) didn't have to look too far.

"Justine Vogel, our CFO at the time, was the logical next step," said Crane. "So why go through the process and upheaval of bringing in an outside third party when you have someone who has been here for more than 13 years. I had no problem with it and encouraged it. You water the flower, fertilize it and then let it grow."

Goodman agreed, "Justine, as the CFO of this community, consistently received the highest scores of any department head from the residents. So you have someone with the financial mind that she has, the knowledge of the community and who at the same time has the confidence of the residents...well, this points to someone with the necessary leadership and personal skills to

ABOVE As RiverWoods grew, so did the community outreach and fund-raising efforts through their gala, held every two years for a different local nonprofit.
BELOW Henry Hood, Woods resident and Chair of the Resident Council, personally met with every new Ridge resident to welcome them.
RIGHT Justine Vogel became CEO in 2007.

be our new CEO and lead the organization into the future. Who better?"

The only problem, Vogel wasn't so sure they were right. "I thought they were crazy when they asked me, because at the time I was only 36 and really didn't feel like I was ready to take such a big step," she said.

Not to worry, Crane and Goodman—as well as the Board and Resident Council—weren't going to just drop her into the deep end of the pool. After she found it in herself to accept the opportunity, she worked with Crane and Goodman through a period of transition. "There was no doubt she would make it, though she had to become a bit more mellow," said Crane. "I gave her as much support as I could, but I also got out of the way and didn't look over her shoulder to let her make decisions without me second guessing them. There may have been a few things I would have done differently, but everything she did always worked out well."

Goodman adds, "When we promoted Justine to CEO, we knew we had made a good management choice and also had someone who believed in the culture."

By April, 2007, the transition was complete. Vogel had proved beyond anyone's doubt that she was more than capable of managing RiverWoods in all of its

joy, complexity and challenges. On April 30, Crane officially stepped down as CEO. "I am very proud that we turned RiverWoods into something that everyone is very proud of," he said. "RiverWoods was a pure delight to work in and my favorite role."

No one could have known the extent to which the community, its finances and leadership would be tested in the next few years.

THE DARKEST, COLD NIGHT

Back in 2005, RiverWoods was on sound financial footing. However, it wasn't out of the woods yet (pardon the pun).

One of the primary concerns that led RiverWoods to build The Ridge was latent demand for Continuing Care Retirement Communities (CCRCs) on the Seacoast of New Hampshire. Taking up that demand by offering more people the opportunity to live at RiverWoods, they could prevent the possibility of a large competitor with deep pockets taking root.

However, they soon discovered that while The Ridge ate up some of that latent demand, there was still plenty of additional demand in the market. Perhaps the most notable proof was the speed at which The Ridge filled as well as the resumption of a long waiting list for spaces in The Woods and The Ridge.

ABOVE The ad campaign for The Ridge featured profiles of the Priority List members, such as Ellie and Ron Bernasconi, who moved in as soon as The Ridge opened.
BELOW The Ridge residents developed strong connections as the community filled quickly.
RIGHT Bill O'Hanlon of LeCesse Construction (who built The Ridge) and Mike Mondoux, RiverWoods Facilities Manager, walked multiple stakeholders through the land being discussed for The Boulders.

"The Ridge was phenomenally successful," said Goodman. "We sold out much sooner than we thought and stabilized occupancy much more quickly than we thought. That's when we said, we have to use the other 60 acres that we bought when building The Ridge and had not yet developed. We decided we had to build The Boulders."

Though they had a gut feeling a new campus would succeed, the Board again did their homework. "We did a market study to investigate the merits of building on the property we owned," said Bob Lietz, who at that time was Chairman of the Strategic Planning Committee and a Board member since 2004. "The market study came back positive that we could build the type of campus we envisioned and fill it up in a reasonable amount of time."

The other reason to build The Boulders, said Vogel, "We obviously have something very good here and part of our mission is to provide our way of life to more people, while securing greater financial stability."

Even though many Board members, employees and residents—especially at The Woods—had been through expansion before, there were still objections from within the RiverWoods community.

Of course, there were some residents concerned that another expansion would alter the community and cause RiverWoods to lose its' tightknit feeling. And there were also those concerned that another campus would put the larger community at financial risk.

One Ridge resident said he thought it was a Ponzi scheme. Another seconded that by arguing that RiverWoods would use the entrance fees from The Ridge to fund new building. Another worried that they felt settled in their new home and happy with the size of their community, but would now have many more neighbors and the disturbance of nearby construction.

But overall, the residents' frame of mind is summed in a December, 2007, issue of

"We obviously have something very good here and part of our mission is to provide our way of life to more people while securing greater financial stability."

JUSTINE VOGEL

The "Road to Nowhere" which eventually became The Boulders campus.

The RiverWoods Reporter, "As residents, we are gratefully benefitting from the decisions and work of previous trustees and employees. Most of us are happy to be here and our opposition, if there is any, to building [a new campus] is not because we are selfish or self-satisfied; if problems of the road, medical care, staffing and the like could be resolved, we would be happy to welcome additional friends."

The first step toward soothing concerns was more a matter of altering perceptions than of substance. Initially, the new campus was to be called The Ridge Expansion, which felt uncomfortable for those at The Ridge who wanted to maintain a small community. This was quickly, if not inadvertently solved by changing the name to The Boulders.

To allay financial concerns, Justine and her team undertook an education campaign with the Board, residents and staff, similar to when The Ridge was built. Many meetings were held with all three groups, and the feasibility study was shared with them, to demonstrate the existing unmet demand. The RiverWoods leadership also reviewed the fiscal rationale; with additional residents, the costs of operation would be spread among more people. Another advantage was that a third campus would be a strong, proactive move against potential competition.

To mitigate concerns over construction and increased traffic flow, the design team routinely met with Ridge residents to resolve residents' issues. These discussions led to a number of compromises over the design of the new campus and the existing Ridge roadways.

In the end, nearly everyone within RiverWoods was satisfied and ready to move forward. As Bob Shealor, an early resident of The Ridge, put it, "I'll tell you one thing, everyone had a lot of confidence in Justine to pull us through and manage it. The one complaint I do have is that the town gave us hell. The Planning Board really put it to us."

Ridge resident Lorraine Graham agreed, "We had a hard time at every stage, even though we are the biggest taxpayer in town, but we worked with them and made some very big concessions."

In fact, RiverWoods did all it could to keep the town and its neighbors happy. Tom Adams, another resident of The Ridge, noted, "I think the people of Exeter realize that we contribute a lot and we did bend over backwards to be good neighbors. We put up trees, significantly altered the streets we would build, and really did everything we

ABOVE The increased number of RiverWoods residents had a positive impact on the downtown Exeter retail community.
BELOW Sheila Francoeur, five-term New Hampshire State representative, joins the Board.
RIGHT Raymond Goodman and Bob Beecher, Board members, chat with Carol Knapp, Woods resident, at a Board/resident holiday party.

could to compromise and keep people happy."

During this time period, Raymond Goodman retired from the Board in February of 2008 and handed the reins to Vice Chairman Bob Lietz. Because Lietz joined the Board in 2004, he didn't have firsthand experience with a RiverWoods development project from start to finish. However, he had seen the final preparations for completing construction and moving residents in.

An attorney, Bob was the co-founder of Rye Capital Management and at the time of his Board Chairmanship was a senior executive with AAI, Inc. His shrewd and methodical mind coupled with a warmth for residents and

a passion for the RiverWoods mission would prove invaluable as the community faced one of its greatest challenges.

At about this same time, the Board also gained a seasoned negotiator, five-term New Hampshire State Representative, Sheila Francoeur. During her time in the state legislature, Francoeur served as Speaker Pro Tem, House Majority Whip and Chairman of the Commerce Committee. She also served on the Rules Committee, the Legislation Administration Committee and was Chairman of The Rockingham County Delegation. To say the least, she was a smart and politically savvy addition to the Board.

THE FLOOR FALLS OUT

Initial discussion about The Boulders began soon after The Ridge was opened, but it wasn't until almost three years later, in late August of 2008 that RiverWoods received approvals from the Exeter Zoning and Planning boards to move ahead on the project. As Francoeur wryly noted, "There are no express trains here. They're all locals."

The three years had not been wasted, however. An aggressive marketing campaign was launched, which included a series of educational sessions for prospective residents to introduce them to the concept of the CCRC. The sessions were held both on the RiverWoods campus, and in nearby New Hampshire and Massachusetts towns. By June 2008, increase. This, in turn, sparked massive losses for a number of banks around the country, in

> **Yesterday the Dow closed up 890 points to close at just under 9100. Today the Fed may cut rates 50 or 75 bps – may even go lower than 1%. Crazy times. I've even done some praying.**

FROM JUSTINE VOGEL'S DAILY JOURNAL

RiverWoods had secured 80 percent pre-sales. With the town approval coming through in late August, RiverWoods was finally positioned to begin the bond issuance process that September.

The Board voted unanimously to move forward. Dawn Barker, Vice President of Human Resources, was selected for the role of Project Manager for The Boulders. She would receive support from Mark Hepp, an external consultant. They worked with JSA Architects, who designed the Ridge, to plan the new community. The future for the small nonprofit looked bright. But storm clouds had been gathering nationally, and that would change the outlook quickly.

As many will recall, August of 2008 was not a good year to be in the real-estate development business. Beginning as early as 2007, the subprime mortgage market was failing fast as more and more homeowners were unable to make regular payments and foreclosures began to

particular the titans of Wall Street.

In April 2007, subprime mortgage lender New Century Financial filed for bankruptcy. In July, Bear Stearns liquidated two hedge funds that had invested heavily in securities backed by subprime mortgage loans. In August, American Home Mortgage Investment went belly up and Countrywide Financial, which in 2006 had financed 20 percent of all mortgages in the U.S., had its credit rating cut by Fitch Ratings to its third lowest investment rating.

By 2008, the U.S. economy was in a real-estate-driven recession causing home sales and home values to plummet. In March, the U.S. government backed up Bear Stearns and guided its sale to JPMorgan Chase. In September, Lehman Brothers filed for bankruptcy, which proved to be the tipping point that drove the real-estate market and global financial markets into a tailspin. The U.S. and the world were plunged into the worst recession

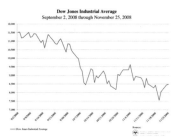

ABOVE A three month snapshot of the Dow Jones Industrial Average. **BELOW & RIGHT** The stock market crash of 2008 happened at the exact moment RiverWoods was finalizing their funding to build The Boulders.

since the Great Depression.

As Vogel remembers, "By August of 2008, we thought we were home free. We had our approvals from the town, we'd resolved the issues with our neighbors, we had more than 80 percent of the units pre-sold and we had two banks who had agreed to provide a letter of credit to establish liquidity support so we could issue our bonds.

"Then two weeks later, Lehman Brothers files for bankruptcy. After that, one of our two letter of credit banks backed out at the last minute. It wasn't because they'd lost faith in us, but they were having their own troubles at the time.

"We were in a world of hurt and left wondering what we should do. The lending markets had gone crazy, interest rates were skyrocketing, we needed a second bank to be a letter of credit bank and by this point we had already spent about $5 million."

This tipping point meant not only that RiverWoods may not have been able to get the financing it needed. The crash also affected each of the 80 prospective residents. They'd put 10% down of the entrance fee for presale with the majority of them counting on selling their homes to pay the remaining 90 percent. Suddenly, their houses were not worth nearly what they were two months prior.

"If people can't sell their homes or the homes are worth significantly less, they won't be able to move in. We are a housing concern so we were right in the thick of the bursting of the real-estate bubble. We had to decide if we should move forward with the financing, for which we would be obligated and build the property, or hold off," said Lietz.

"The biggest challenge was that the answers to how this would work out and what would happen next with the economy were about a year-and-a-half away. By then, we would be $70 million into The Boulders for which we and our residents would be obligated. That was the crux of the debate," he continued.

As Toomey noted, "This was a real dark night of the soul for the Board and RiverWoods."

Lietz called for the Finance Committee to meet in early October to examine these questions. Meanwhile, Vogel and Kevin Goyette, RiverWoods CFO, started looking to replace the bank that backed out. They also started developing strategies for moving forward, as well as taking a closer look at the feasibility studies and RiverWoods' overall financial picture.

"We met with our finance committee and worked through the options; many weren't good," said Vogel. "After about a month of non-stop work, Kevin got a second

ABOVE & BELOW The enormous challenge of 2008 was to protect the lifestyle of the current RiverWoods residents (above, Tom and Mimi Adams) and fulfill the promise to the prospective residents (below, Steve and Romie Walker). **RIGHT** Bob Lietz, Chair of the Board of Trustees, led the crucial decision-making process that the Board followed.

bank on board for our bond sale. Then we went to our Board and said, 'Here's what we want to do. We have the financing in line. We have the pre-sales. We believe that if we do this now, nobody else in our industry is going to be entering the market with a new development...Nobody else will have the ability or the guts to do it at this time.' We also knew that the demand for what we offer, our unique way, would not fall apart. It would be a challenge, but we could do it."

As Francoeur remembers, "One of the great strengths of our Board is that we all share the mission of the organization and we always want to achieve the best outcome. It was not ego-driven or a glamour Board where you do it to be seen and demonstrate you are a good person. Now, I don't want people to think there aren't people on the Board who don't have egos. I would say we all have those. But for some reason, egos are left at the door and we function in a very collaborative way."

This strength would prove to be a decisive element in the October 2008 Board meeting where a final decision had to be made. "I remember that meeting and in credit to Bob, our Chair, he wanted to be sure everyone at the meeting was heard and if they had any fears they could express them," said Francoeur. "We all had fears because of the unknowns,

such as, would our marketing team be able to sell the units and would these prospective residents be able to sell their homes in a timely manner and move in? Would moving forward jeopardize the people who already live at The Ridge and The Woods?"

Lietz adds, "Everyone at that meeting spoke, maybe hesitantly at first, but spoke of moving on because of the stage we were already at. We were already $5 million into it and at 82 percent for presales. The Board looked at all of the information we had, which included plans put together by Kevin and Justine as well as information based on the due diligence done by the banks backing us. The Board said we have people who have made a commitment to us and are counting on us moving forward.

"At that Board meeting the senior management team was very effective at coming in and saying we could get The Boulders built and filled up based on their evaluation of the situation. And the fact that the banks were behind us was heartening because they'd done their due diligence and believed we would succeed. We had a lot of faith in Kevin and Cathleen to make it happen.

"Also, nothing had changed from our market study. We still felt we are a desired location and there was still going to be strong demand for this type of living."

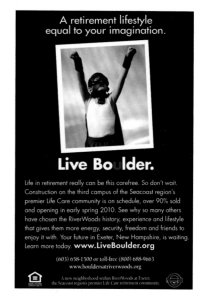

ABOVE The Boulders marketing effort included print, on-line, and in-person events.
RIGHT "We wanted our Priority Members to feel they were moving into a community and have a sense of belonging before it was even built." Cathleen Toomey, Vice President of Marketing

Naming The Boulders

To say the least, The Boulders earned its name not from the geography, but the geology of the site. As Raymond Goodman, Board of Trustees chair at the time, remembers, "During the Ice Age, as the glaciers receded they left a moraine behind, essentially a collection of boulders scattered about as debris. So when we went to do the first site analysis I thought, 'Oh my God this is going to cost way too much' because there are all of these gigantic boulders, boulders as big as a house lying around.

"As I drove away I began to see that we could incorporate the geological features into the building and landscaping and called Justine right away, and I said, 'Justine, the name has to be The Boulders.'"

That became one of the names that we circulated to the current RiverWoods residents, who voted and debated about a variety of names, until, ultimately, the authenticity of The Boulders name won the day.

"The grassroots effort that led to the creation of RiverWoods illustrates the Granite State spirit and demonstrates the strength and resiliency that define us as a place and a people." GOVERNOR MAGGIE HASSAN

Justine Vogel; Maggie Hassan, Current New Hampshire Governor and former State Senator; Maryanna Hatch and Rosemary Coffin at the November 2008 groundbreaking during a torrential, cold rain.

A formal groundbreaking ceremony followed the vote. RiverWoods hosted nearly all of the 80 families who'd signed on to become residents of The Boulders. The celebration also included current residents, co-founders Maryanna Hatch and Rosemary Coffin and local dignitaries, which included Gov. Maggie Hassan who was the State Senator for Exeter at the time. Held outside in November, celebrants suffered through a drenching rainstorm with 40-mile-an-hour winds. "Nothing was simple about this project," Vogel said, "but the tent didn't blow over, so we figured we would be ok."

THE WORK BEGINS

Within a few weeks of the Board vote, the bond sale went forward and RiverWoods successfully gained the financing it needed to build The Boulders. "We were about the last CCRC to get major financing for a year-and-a-half," said Lietz. "We just made it because things got worse and worse as the winter went on... Financing literally dried up for these types of entities."

With ground being broken, the marketing team had to ensure there were residents to fill the new campus. To accomplish this daunting task, they engaged in a multi-faceted strategy. The first piece was determining the scope of the challenge ahead.

"We created what Justine called The 1984 Report and I called The Stop Light Report, where we dug down into each prospect and examined what the individual barriers were to them selling their homes and moving in," said Toomey. "Then we came up with strategies to help bring those barriers down. We stayed on top of this data and developed more systems to track our sales than we'd ever had in the history of RiverWoods and we still use those systems today."

Vogel adds, "We also worked to develop strong relationships with our prospective residents prior to even finishing the building. What we were hearing in the industry was that other communities that had been financed only a few years earlier and were opening in 2008 were experiencing massive cancellations. People were calling these other communities and saying 'We can't come. Give us our money back.'

"We realized that what is different about our community is once you are part of the community and understand what it's all about, you never want to not be part of it. So we created a program called 'Friends of The Boulders' where existing residents became a pen pal with an incoming Boulders resident to establish a relationship. The pen pals met at events we held for prospective and incoming

ABOVE Rosemary, David Coffin and Maryanna Hatch get front row seats at the Boulders groundbreaking ceremony.
BELOW Maryanna Hatch and Cathleen Toomey share a hug as the ceremony concludes.
RIGHT Justine Vogel references the 'monsoon' and the resilience of the 130 people under the quaking tent.

"We were about the last CCRC to get major financing for a year and a half. We just made it."

BOB LIETZ, CHAIRMAN OF THE BOARD

Construction begins on The Boulders in 2008.

residents as well as kept in touch through email and so on."

Toomey adds, "We wanted people at The Boulders to feel they were moving into a community and to have a sense of belonging before it was even built. That's why you hear stories from Boulders residents that they snuck in to look at where they would live as the construction was happening. We brought depositors through The Boulders as it was being built. In order to help them visualize their space, we spray painted names onto the floor of their chosen apartment."

Additionally, if tracking showed a prospective resident wavering in their commitment, the team started recruiting a new person so they were never waiting for a cancellation decision. "We were cultivating more people to come so we had more people than we needed to move in," said Toomey. "The reality was that someone could walk away at any time and get their money back. They could walk away the day they were going to move in, so we were prepared if that should happen."

"Justine was never satisfied with the amount of information she had," said Toomey. "She wanted more and more and we had to do more and more reports and then take them to the Board so they could see what we were doing

ABOVE To help incoming Boulders residents visualize their apartments, their names and apartment numbers were sprayed on the concrete.
RIGHT Construction began during a particularly cold winter so that the building would be ready within 18 months.

and how well it was working. This also allowed them to ask questions and make suggestions so the whole process was as collaborative as we could make it."

For those incoming residents having trouble selling their homes, RiverWoods established a relationship with a local bank to offer bridge loans until their homes sold. Goyette and Toomey were able to work out a plan that benefitted both RiverWoods and the prospective resident by offering options to help them move in, even if they had trouble selling their home.

In the end, it worked. The Boulders opened in March of 2010, and three months later, achieved 80 percent occupancy, in one of the most challenging real estate markets. It was a huge success.

Additionally, the project came in on time and under budget due to the oversight of Barker and Hepp.

"We were blessed with a fantastic project team – the economy was awful and that created some difficult situations, but the team never wavered," said Barker.

Sheila Francoeur, who was a member of the Board/Resident Construction Oversight Committee, said "To say the least, we moved ahead only after holding a full examination and discussion and it worked."

Vogel adds, "I think my favorite thing about that whole process, if you can have a favorite thing

about such a dark time, was that our full team came together to ensure our success. From Kevin moving mountains to get the financing completed, to Cathleen tracking prospects to ensure we had the move-ins, to Dawn managing the design and construction...it involved the majority of our senior team and we were all working to ensure RiverWoods' continued success."

As The Boulders development played out, RiverWoods did not forget about the rest of the organization. As many other organizations during the recession were slashing budgets and laying off staff, RiverWoods looked at creative solutions even as investment income fell off. "We went back and examined how we funded operations and looked at ways to cut costs so we didn't have to rely upon our investment income to help fund operations," said Lietz. "We knew we needed to be less dependent on things outside of our control for funding.

"We did put a pay freeze in place for 2009 and into fiscal year 2010, but we didn't cut our staff or services. And, we only had a normal increase in fees. Since then, we have even managed to reduce the rate of our annual fee increases, which is a product of the financial stability we have achieved through the three campuses. Basically, costs are spread among a greater number

ABOVE A jubilant Maryanna Hatch is at the center of her third RiverWoods ribbon cutting.
CENTER Board member Sheila Francoeur, Maryanna Hatch and Sue and Dick Kaplan, the first two Boulders residents to move in, at the opening ceremony.
BELOW The Boulders hosted one of RiverWoods' gala fundraisers.
RIGHT Maryanna gives the keynote address at The Boulders' ribbon cutting ceremony.

Dot Bell and Andy O'Book,
Woods residents work in the
raised garden beds.

Don't Wait Until It's Too Late...

Many people nearing retirement age do not understand the concept of a CCRC. For CCRCs in general, and RiverWoods in particular, moving to either The Woods, The Ridge or The Boulders is the equivalent of expanding your opportunities, allowing yourself to continue to grow intellectually and personally and increasing your ability to truly enjoy your retirement years.

However, people all too often wait until it's too late to take advantage of everything RiverWoods has to offer. This point is not lost on Boulders resident John Perreca, "Coming to RiverWoods isn't like saying you are ready to stop living. You are saying 'I want more from my life.'

"Many of us understand that one of the most important issues you have to be aware of when it comes to real estate is location, location, location. With RiverWoods, you need to be aware of timing, timing and timing. This is the crux of the decision to come to RiverWoods.

"Most people wait too long to where they are no longer healthy and a CCRC is not able to take them because the cost is prohibitive. I have had the disappointing experience of trying to convince friends to come here and they stalled and stalled. One friend's wife found out that due to her husband's Alzheimer's he forgot to pay a premium on long-term care insurance and the insurance was cancelled. Because of this, the issue of timing was brought to me in a very tragic and personal way.

"So please, don't wait until it's too late. Life is good and there is a lot of life here."

ABOVE Sheila and John Welch, Boulders residents, enjoy a meal with John and Mary Beth Gillespie, Woods residents.
BELOW Glenn Klink, Chairman of RiverWoods Board of Trustees through 2014.

of residents, so The Boulders helped stabilize things even more. Currently, our rate of increase on monthly service fees is the lowest it has been in 20 years."

At the grand opening ceremony for The Boulders, Exeter Town Manager Russ Dean said, "RiverWoods provides a stable employment base for the town that's made it one of our top five employers. It cannot be stressed enough, particularly in this day and age, how important it is for communities to have strong, stable employers, particularly those that can offer jobs to young people.

"In recent years, the town of Exeter has made this kind of development a priority and the vision of those involved with RiverWoods have made this a reality. It is nothing short of a genuinely amazing accomplishment."

2010 AND FORWARD

After opening, The Boulders, along with The Woods and The Ridge, continued to strengthen. By June of 2012, the day that Lietz stepped down as chair of the Board of Trustees, The Boulders hit 100 percent occupancy. An incredible accomplishment when one considers the degree of uncertainty and economic destruction wrought on other organizations and families by the recession of 2008/2009.

As America and much of the world from an economic and social standpoint fell silent, RiverWoods, a kitchen table creation founded by a small group of dedicated people, flourished. As Lietz noted, the success of The Boulders and RiverWoods at large is a reflection of the cultural architecture of RiverWoods...the Three Legged Stool, as Crane so famously called it.

In 2012, Lietz believed that after eight years on the board, four of them as chair, it was time to allow someone else with a new set of ideas, a new sense of direction for the future to take over. "Glenn Klink had demonstrated a real affinity for the organization," Lietz said, "and had been on the Board for five years, so he had developed a very good working knowledge of the organization. He also had the willingness to put the time and effort into the role...

he embraced that opportunity. So he was a natural fit and was unanimously elected to be Chair."

Klink, who was then Chair of the Strategic Planning Committee, also brought leadership expertise to the role from his more than 30 years as a leader in both the hospital and insurance industries.

Almost immediately, Klink, the Board, staff and residents of RiverWoods set themselves to the task of maintaining and improving all they had created. "It's a continuous state of community building and transitions," said Klink. "The primary question is how do we keep the campuses fresh and exciting so they don't lose their appeal. They each have their own feel and identity and they all must be maintained and strengthened so they continue to flourish."

Vogel adds, "When we prepare our goals every year we put them into three concentric circles: protect the core, plan for the future and maximize our resources. It is our belief that if you are not maximizing your resources you are not protecting the core; if you're not planning for the future, you're not protecting the core. Some organizations would look at their accomplishments and the risks ahead and put their head in the sand and close ranks and say we are just going to do this and only this forever.

"We believe you have to plan for the future to protect what you have and you have to make sure you are doing it in an efficient way to protect what you have.

"Some of that is financial, but some of that is about why we are here, what is our mission, what is our vision.....how do we continue to provide community and peace of mind and build on that? Remember, as an organization, we were founded on persistence. It's in our genes."

Lietz is confident RiverWoods will continue to find its way. "Glenn and Justine, and the others, the Three Legged Stool, have done a wonderful job of doing this...of helping RiverWoods begin its next 20 years."

ABOVE Helen Armstrong in one of the two Woods art studios.
RIGHT Mary Avery, Boulders resident, is caught in a gardening moment. (top)
Boulders residents Claire McQuade, her dog Buddy, and John Secor, who met at RiverWoods, share a walk along the river. (center)
Woods resident John Morgenthau in his workshop perfecting one of his prized wood bowls. (bottom)

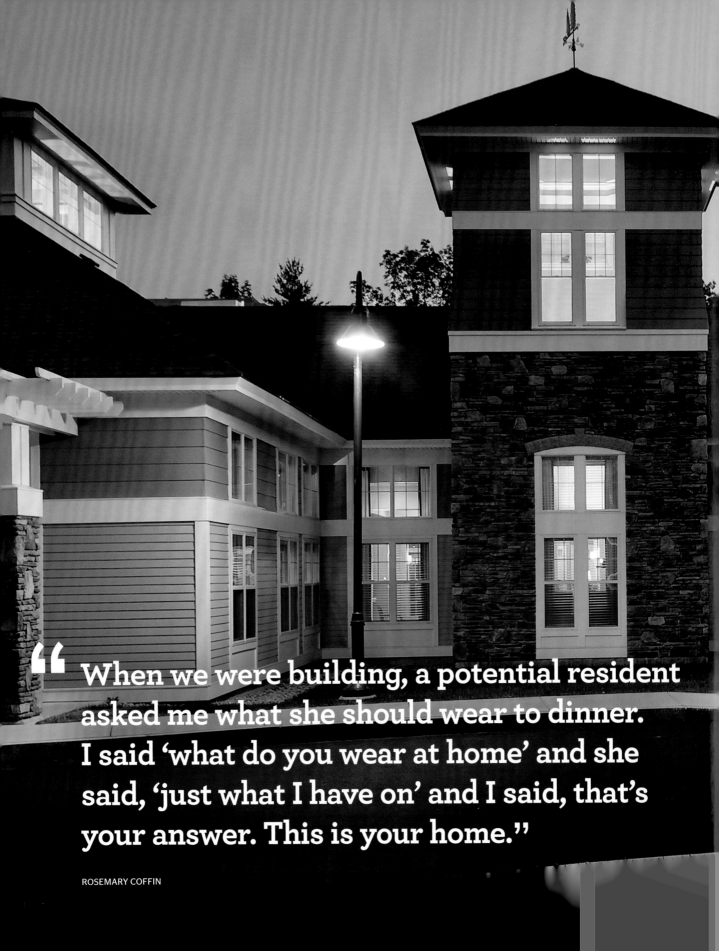

"When we were building, a potential resident asked me what she should wear to dinner. I said 'what do you wear at home' and she said, 'just what I have on' and I said, that's your answer. This is your home."

ROSEMARY COFFIN

"I say to my friends, please don't wait until it's too late. There's a lot of life here."

JOHN PERRECA, BOULDERS RESIDENT

Residents and staff gather in the Wood Great Bay room in 2002.

Dot and John Perreca, with their dog in the RiverWoods trails. Dot is a second generation RiverWoods resident.

It's About Community

Afterword

By 2014 the organization had reached maturity in Exeter. The combination of the three campuses, each with their own flavor and personality, combined with a seasoned management team, had really taken shape. RiverWoods moved to a management structure designed around the concept of "local ownership." That concept encouraged the resident service leadership and management teams of the Woods, Ridge and Boulders to set the style and personality of their campuses, while still operating under the overarching culture of transparency, teamwork and community.

Meanwhile, the Board of Trustees had been engaged in a five year process to develop a more formal corporate structure. They did this because they knew that future growth in Exeter was unlikely; yet knew they had a vision to serve more people in a broader geographic, and hopefully, broader demographic, range. They also wanted to create a way to serve that vision, while minimizing undo financial risk to the existing campuses. The culmination of their work came with the formation of The RiverWoods Group in 2013, to be the parent and "sole member" of RiverWoods at Exeter. As future growth is evaluated, The RiverWoods Group structure will bring ideas to life.

Over the past 20 years, RiverWoods has grown from one campus to three, from serving 250 residents at a time to over 600 and from employing 150 staff members to 470. Many things have changed, but the one constant is our commitment to community. That commitment is evident in the every day life of residents and staff, in their interactions and true affection for both the community and one another.

Justine Vogel

Justine Vogel,
RiverWoods President and CEO
January 2014

Trustees

1994 to 2014

Index

1pm - Signag

- Main Entrance -

Cedar Stained fike
12" & 9" letters
1 ground "nash
gate signe → ~~XXXXX~~
<u>Receiving</u> - Monadn

→ Main Entrance -
Information Cente

Monadnock . ~~$~~
Handicapped -
Check @ KCs for ng